PRAISE

It's hard to imagine a book more i
people trade away nearly everythi
artificial identity, Cary Schmidt stands at the crossroads to offer the reader something infinitely better—real identity and purpose from our Creator. I couldn't put
this book down!

MARK HOOVER
Lead Pastor, NewSpring Church, Wichita, KS

Understanding who we are and whose we are is fundamental to following Jesus on
mission in this world. Too many of us walk around trying to be someone we are not,
to prove our worth to people whose admiration can't fill our hearts in ways only
Jesus can. And there are too many cheap substitutes for affirmation and identity that
only disappoint. This is why Cary Schmidt's work is a welcome, refreshing respite for
weary Christians tired of proving themselves, striving for illusory approval. Schmidt
points us to the warm embrace of our heavenly Father and the empowering and
liberating vision of what it means to find our identity in the One who made us.

DANIEL DARLING
Senior VP of NRB; pastor and author of several books, including
The Dignity Revolution, The Characters of Christmas, and *A Way With Words*

Raw, honest and extremely helpful. Every Christian needs to come to terms with
what Cary came to terms with; he has the scars and testimony and shares with us here.
This is life-altering stuff in the most positive way.

RON EDMONDSON
Pastor, author, consultant at RonEdmondson.com

What if we stopped trying so hard to please others? What if we discovered the way
to find the joy and peace that comes from discovering our identity in Christ? In *Stop
Trying,* Cary Schmidt does a masterful job of showing the transformation of the
followers of Jesus so we might understand the path for our transformation as well.

THOM S. RAINER
Founder and CEO, Church Answers;
author of *Where Have All the Church Members Gone?*

Wow! Please walk this journey! Words fly off the page and into your mind as if your
own heart wrote them. We all hurt the same . . . and need the same remedy: God's
presence.

MELINDA CAZIS
Pastor's wife, mom, college professor, Christian in NYC

In *Stop Trying*, Cary Schmidt has uncovered the real issue of identity crisis, which includes a cultural form of identity theft that we inflict upon ourselves. Our true identity in Christ prunes away the high maintenance identities that we've crafted, allowing for growth and genuine satisfaction. This book leads to something better than the best life—it helps the readers to have *abundant* lives in Christ.

FRANCIE TAYLOR
Keep the Heart LLC

On the path to seeing ourselves as God sees us, Cary Schmidt is a trustworthy guide. With clear language, engaging stories, and rich biblical insights, *Stop Trying* will lead you into a fresh encounter with the gospel. By focusing on Christ, Cary shows us, our true selves come into focus. This is a message of hope for all of us.

RYAN LOKKESMOE
Pastor and author of *Paul and His Team: What the Early Church Can Teach Us about Leadership and Influence*

With refreshing transparency and biblical clarity, Cary explains the wonderful liberty of simply resting in Jesus. How I wish that my younger "performance driven" self could have read *Stop Trying* thirty years ago! You will come away from this book freshly astounded by the grace of God and refreshingly energized by what Jesus is doing in your life.

KURT SKELLY
Pastor of Faith Baptist Church, Fredericksburg, VA

Discover the real struggle in life, why it matters, and what to do about it! This book unmasks the empty life, stands you in front of a mirror, and helps you see the beautiful "you" that God has created in Christ. This book takes you on a radical journey that will transform and ground you.

RAYMOND CAZIS
Pastor of International Baptist Church, Brooklyn, NY

Stop Trying answers some of the most pressing identity questions of our time with the clarity of the gospel. It will invite you to embrace your gospel identity and experience the peace that comes from living out who you were created to be in everyday, practical ways. I absolutely agree with this book!

SCOTT TEWELL
Pastor of Rosedale Baptist Church, Rosedale, MD

This is a compelling and deeply transformational book! Imagine having an identity that is durable no matter what life throws at you. In *Stop Trying*, Cary Schmidt unmasks the weak identity structures of our culture, and replaces them with the only strong identity option. This book will set you free to grow into and live out of who you really are.

JOHNNY HUNT
Sr. Vice President of Evangelism and Leadership, North American Mission Board
Former Sr. Pastor, First Baptist Church of Woodstock, GA
Former president of the Southern Baptist Convention

How to Receive
—Not Achieve—
Your Real Identity

STOP TRYING

CARY SCHMIDT

MOODY PUBLISHERS | CHICAGO

Published in association with agent Cynthia Ruchti with Books & Such Literary Management.

Edited by Amanda Cleary Eastep
Interior and cover design: Erik M. Peterson
Cover illustration of man looking up copyright © 2018 by Serhii Borodin/iStock (1072415440). All rights reserved.

All websites and phone numbers listed herein are accurate at the time of publication but may change in the future or cease to exist. The listing of website references and resources does not imply publisher endorsement of the site's entire contents. Groups and organizations are listed for informational purposes, and listing does not imply publisher endorsement of their activities.

Library of Congress Cataloging-in-Publication Data

Names: Schmidt, Cary, author.
Title: Stop trying : how to receive --not achieve--your real identity / Cary Schmidt.
Description: Chicago : Moody Publishers, [2021] | Includes bibliographical references. | Summary: "In Stop Trying you'll understand why defining your identity outside of Jesus Christ is ultimately fragile, hollow, and unsatisfying. Become grounded in theology and delight in a dynamic relationship with Jesus Christ that helps you know who you are by knowing Him"-- Provided by publisher.
Identifiers: LCCN 2020031946 (print) | LCCN 2020031947 (ebook) | ISBN 9780802419989 (paperback) | ISBN 9780802498892 (ebook)
Subjects: LCSH: Identity (Psychology)--Religious aspects--Christianity.
Classification: LCC BV4509.5 .S325 2021 (print) | LCC BV4509.5 (ebook) | DDC 248.4--dc23
LC record available at https://lccn.loc.gov/2020031946
LC ebook record available at https://lccn.loc.gov/2020031947

Originally delivered by fleets of horse-drawn wagons, the affordable paperbacks from D. L. Moody's publishing house resourced the church and served everyday people. Now, after more than 125 years of publishing and ministry, Moody Publishers' mission remains the same—even if our delivery systems have changed a bit. For more information on other books (and resources) created from a biblical perspective, go to www.moodypublishers.com or write to:

Moody Publishers
820 N. LaSalle Boulevard
Chicago, IL 60610

1 3 5 7 9 10 8 6 4 2

Printed in the United States of America

To My Wife, Dana—
I love you, and thank you for sharing life with me
and for vividly showing me a beautiful gospel identity.

CONTENTS

Part One

LOSING

*"For whoever would save his life will lose it,
but whoever loses his life for my sake and
the gospel's will save it."*

JESUS IN MARK 8:35

WHAT COMES NEXT when the life we've tried to achieve proves un-fulfilling?

What happens when painful events disrupt our hearts and we lose our sense of self? How do we discover our truest and most durable selves in such a fragile world?

Times of loss can be the starting point of a new journey, and the most transformational spiritual journeys are those in which God opens our eyes to new understanding. He shines light into unexplored places of our hearts and gently, wonderfully, rede-fines and reshapes us. He moves the gospel from our heads to our hearts during a lifetime of following Him.

In these pages, I invite you into the discovery of your truest identity. Together, we will merely scratch the surface. There are a billion diamonds in this mine. I can only show you the few that I've seen, but hopefully our short time together will launch you on a lifetime of uncovering the infinite heart of God for you.

Our conversation begins with identity loss. So, let's start digging right here.

Chapter 1

TRYING HARD

Reckoning with Life's Deepest Loss

"Behold, what manner of love the Father hath
bestowed upon us, that we should be called
the sons of God."

1 JOHN 3:1 (KJV)

A THREE-HOUR TREK transported us from the desert of Southern California to the ski slopes of Bear Mountain. It was my son Larry's senior year of high school. We had cleared the schedule for a couple of days of skiing, cherishing time together before the fast-paced spring would lead to his graduation.

We arrived shortly after the ski lifts opened that day, secured our rental gear, and headed for the slopes. We anticipated non-stop fun in a beautiful setting, sharing one of our favorite father-son activities.

Just off the lift on our first run, we paused to adjust our gear and get our bearings. It didn't take Larry long, but the muscle loss in my legs due to chemo treatments during the past year's battle with cancer made me feel as if I were skiing on matchsticks. *I'm going to have to go easy this trip,* I thought to myself. I hoped Larry wouldn't think his recovering dad was slowing him down.

Just over a ridge, a few hundred yards down the slope, I paused to wait for Larry. He wasn't far behind me on his snowboard when we'd started down the run. Now, several minutes passed, and still no Larry. I assumed he was resetting his bindings or adjusting his gear.

Ten minutes. Still no Larry. As I grudgingly knelt to remove my skis in order to begin the laborious climb back up the ridge to check on him, he finally came into view. Before I could ask what took him so long, he slowed to a stop next to me and sat down, breathless.

"I fell and hit my head."

He sounded matter-of-fact and seemed uninjured, so I wasn't too worried. "You're okay?" I asked.

"Yes, but I have a really bad headache. I think I hit my head."

He had told me that already. His repetition was my first warning sign.

"Hey, Dad, how long have we been here?"

I laughed, thinking he was messing with me. He didn't laugh.

"How long do you *think* we've been here, Larry?" My concern was growing.

"I don't know, maybe two days?" He was serious.

He didn't recall that we had arrived only minutes earlier and this was our first trip down the slope. Now I was scared.

"Larry, unstrap your snowboard. We need to get to the first-aid shack right now." We began the long, downhill march, moving slowly to be sure he didn't lose his footing again.

It wasn't long before the medics diagnosed Larry with a serious concussion, declared an end to our ski trip, and sent us to the closest hospital emergency room. The staff rushed us through processing and prepped Larry for an on-the-spot CT scan. The whole ER ordeal took about four hours, during which time Larry's memory worsened and his questions continued with frequent repetition.

It was both alarming and a bit humorous. He seemed fine except for his memory. After doctors calmed my worst fears, I began to entertain both myself and Larry by telling him a different version of the story each time he asked me, "What happened and why are we at the hospital?"

"You ran into a truck."

"I did?"

The next time, I answered, "You plowed into a skier old enough to be your grandmother."

"I did? Is she okay?"

The next, "You attempted a massive ski jump and hurt your head."

On that one he smiled proudly. "I did? Did I get a lot of air?"

Time after time, he asked the same questions. It didn't matter whether I told him the truth or a fiction: he remembered none of it. Finally, the doctors cleared him of serious concerns, gave us care instructions for a severe concussion, and we were sent on our way.

After a short meal, we began the slow drive home with me glancing at my nearly grown son in the passenger's seat. His expression stole my breath. He was clearly trying hard to remember, and migrating toward panic that he couldn't. I slowed and pulled the car to the roadside. Larry's eyes were wild with fear.

"Dad, I don't remember *anything*!"

Larry, typically a quiet, composed individual, is rarely one to express alarm. But in this moment, he was truly terrified.

For all of his trying, he was utterly lost. No recollection of where we were, how long we had been there, how we got there. His growing realization of memory loss overtook him.

What could I say to my son who'd lost all connection to reality? His reference points were gone—his identity was a blur. Psychologically, he was free falling, and no amount of *trying to remember* would help him.

LOSS OF SELF

Something very similar to Larry's memory loss can happen to all of us on spiritual and psychological levels. This kind of traumatic loss involves equally distressing feelings of confusion and helplessness.

First, consider the idea of *loss*. Not all losses are the same. We think of little losses in terms of missing car keys or a lost ball game. We think of big losses in terms of lost relationships, careers, loved ones, financial security, or personal health. The bigger the loss, the more devastating it is, and the deeper it reaches into our psyche, triggering an even deeper loss.

Perhaps one of the most significant losses anyone can face is the *loss of a sense of self*. Something breaks inside of us, and leaves us feeling valueless, meaningless, and hopeless. We wonder if we will ever find our way again.

Have you ever lost your sense of self or faced a time when life made you wonder who you are? *Why* you are? How many times have you asked yourself, *Who am I, really?* Such experiences (on a soul level) are disruptive and alarming to our inner worlds—like a spiritual and emotional concussion.

What can we do when we don't know who we are? Do we sink into despair? Scramble to pull ourselves together and try harder? Do we start over, again and again hoping to magically "get it right" or "find ourselves"? It's confusing and disorienting to face circumstances that leave us asking, "Who am I *now*? Who am I *supposed to be*?"

Ten years ago, I thought I had solid answers to these identity questions, established through hard work over many years. Then, what I thought was solid ground dissolved from under my feet. Circumstances unfolded that evaporated my reference points in life, which left me feeling disoriented and grasping for something to hold onto. A bit like Larry's memory loss, a deep, spiritual loss descended into my heart and mind—a sort of ultimate loss.

This deep loss of self (identity) is psychological, emotional, and spiritual—meaning it impacts our minds, our feelings, and the deepest part of our hearts in complex ways that are intricately interwoven. It triggers a confusing, frightening, spiritual free fall, like being plunged into the deepest part of a murky lake, swimming for the surface, but not being sure which way is up.

That day on the slopes, I knew Larry and I were vulnerable to injury, but I had never considered how vulnerable my soul was to a similar experience. Life hadn't taught me that yet.

Ideally, life goes like this: We work hard in school, graduate, and pursue our dreams. We are told, "You can be whoever you want to be!" Through hard work over several years, we try diligently to build a sense of self—an identity. Then, subconsciously, we tie our hearts to the things we achieve. We come to believe these things define us and give us security and meaning. We draw value and happiness from them. In ways we don't consciously perceive or intend, they begin to own us.

Even when the life work is harder than we expect, we press forward, anticipating that there's a payoff. *Someday, somehow this is going to fulfill and secure me.*

But underneath all the trying, we subconsciously anchor our sense of self to weak things—things that are fragile, losable, and breakable. Knowing we are tied to things that can come undone, we live in subtle fear, trying and hoping to secure our *selves* and avoid deep loss. We bury our fear, tuck our fragility neatly out of sight and mind, and try to secure the self we are constructing. But we know at our core, life is inherently dangerous and can suddenly destabilize and toss us into deep loss.

When identity loss actually unfolds, it is no fun. Losing our fragile selves is painful and emotional. In our desperation for answers and hope, we tend to replace the old "house of cards" with a new one, equally flawed. Scrambling for stability, we look for new places to root our hearts—a new relationship, a new job, a new social media profile, a new people group. We move from one weak place to another. We try on new selves, and each new identity will eventually fail us like the last one.

The cycle repeats itself, unless we break it. But how? Well, that's where God steps in and walks with us into deep loss. He's breaking us free from a broken cycle.

Let me share more about my long walk through deep loss.

FREE FALL—MY SEASON OF LOSS

My most significant experience with identity loss happened twice, and both times it rocked me to the core. It sent me digging for deeper answers and made me eager to understand my "concussion of soul." More importantly, the ultimate loss made me yearn for a primary identity that could never be lost, no matter what life threw at me.

Although I am a pastor, my theology was flawed, and my expectations of God were faulty. My identity was, at least in part, built on weak things. Despite that, God graciously walked with me through a deconstruction of the life I had built *for* Him, and then He put it all back together in a way that sort of blew my mind. The white-hot heat of life events melted the weak and fragile elements of my identity and left me, for the moment, in what felt like that psychological and spiritual "lostness."

Today, I wouldn't trade the journey for anything. One day, you will feel the same way about your loss. But that doesn't stop it from being painful or terrifying right now.

My first loss of self came with a cancer diagnosis. This gave way to months of life-or-death uncertainty, a year of intense treatments, and a couple more years of gradual recovery. After two decades of hard work, my busy pastoral role in a large ministry came to a grinding halt. Unavoidably, I had a new identity—cancer-guy. Chemotherapy and sickness left me incapable of trying and unable to sustain my life roles. That year was filled with many dark hours of asking, "Now, who am I? I can't do or be the things that define me . . . now what?"

The treatments were effective, and cancer went into remission. But restored health merely gave way to a second wave of deep loss. Just when I expected to return to my *normal*, God had other plans. He called our family to follow Him and move away from everything we knew as "familiar" or "secure" and everyone we loved. The call required us to leave twenty-two years of fruitful ministry and flourishing relationships in Southern California. We relocated three thousand miles to Connecticut to serve a small, hurting church family in post-Christian, postmodern New England.

We obeyed Him, though I now regret my early resistance and personal unwillingness. My hesitation to trust and follow God should have been the first warning light on my spiritual dashboard that my identity was more bound up in fragile, temporal things than I ever knew. Too much of my sense of self was tied to my trying and my personal achievements.

In the first loss, God revealed to me how fragile my health is and how temporary I am. In the second, He reminded me how vulnerable and fragile the rest of life is.

It's all losable.

This providential chain of events was a spiritual, emotional, and psychological growth curve as I've never experienced. The next two years became a slow, murky swim, in search of the surface. Strangely, though I was surrounded by loving people, I wrestled internally with that deeper loss of self and feelings of disorientation. *Who am I, now? Who am I supposed to be? What if I am not able to be who others expect me to be?*

I was oblivious to the identity structures that had subtly come to define me over decades, until God lovingly removed them, and replaced them with unfamiliar things. With my identity lost, I felt psychologically lost and dazed, trying hard to remember. It was such a strange experience. As a longtime pastor who had counseled many twenty- and thirtysomethings over the years, intellectually, I knew the answers. Theologically, I could teach the answers. Biblically, I could quote the answers. But personally, in these seasons, I needed to *experience* the answers. What I knew to be true was unavoidably being forced from my head to my heart.

In both losses, my go-to response, at first, was to sit and stare—numbness of soul. There were often tears. My many years of trying to build a solid identity proved fleeting. The questions that had haunted me first in the chemo chair found me again two years later on lonely winter mornings in Dunkin' Donuts.

I sat alone, sipped coffee, and grieved my losses. *Why would God remove my diligently constructed, strong foundation?* Emotionally immersed in a New England winter, I faced overwhelming personal and ministry challenges, and wrestled daily with the desolate thoughts of "Now what? *Why* has God done this, and *where* is it all going?"

To know me during those years, you probably wouldn't have seen the deeper struggle. This was profoundly personal. Through the losses, most moments were not sorrowful, and not every day was gray. There was joy in the midst of grief, thanks to God's patient grace. And the years proved God to be faithful. Beautiful and fruitful outcomes have grown from what seemed to be barren seasons. But it has taken every bit of a decade to understand God's loving and patient deconstruction and reconstruction process of my soul.

Maybe this book will save you some time and give you back some of those years of wondering what God is doing. Maybe it will ignite flickers of hope within you.

SPLINTERVILLE

Identity loss reminds me of the stunning, scale-model boats a friend of mine builds from ultra-thin balsa wood. With scalpel-like precision, he crafts railings, bunk beds, hatches, and fully operational doors from the impossibly thin sheets of fiber. But he tiptoes around his creations because even a stiff breeze could collapse months of microscopic construction. Spilled coffee? It's over. A fist pounded on the table?

Welcome to Splinterville.

Nobody ever took a vacation on a balsa wood boat. The scale model looks good, but it can't float. It is made of fragile materials; it is not designed for the harsh realities of the sea.

Such are many facets of our lives. We live with a similar kind of fragility in our souls. We unknowingly build balsa wood selves. Our psyches are glued-together bits of not-built-to-last materials —health, looks, income, status, ethnicity, accomplishments, relationships, and social media profiles. We are perpetually haunted by comparison, the opinions of others, competition, and fear. We are forever trying to measure up to the world around us. When we do, we feel good. When we fail, we feel loss.

It's all very fragile and vulnerable. It's all extremely weak. One stiff breeze and . . . Splinterville.

We actually believe our balsa wood selves can sail, and we are shocked at the collapse when we attempt to navigate life's rough seas. Sudden loss exposes our identity structures (a term we will explore more later). Balsa wood faith and identities fall apart, and we are confronted with our weak selves and fragile building supplies. Our faith and sense of self are often constructed with faulty, performance-based, try-harder materials. Then life's hardships put us to the test. Jesus' little brother, James, called it the testing or trying of your faith (James 1:3). Too often we are ill-equipped to understand how faith in Jesus informs and transforms our true identity, and therefore unexpected loss jolts us to the core. It reveals how fragile we really are, and how badly we need more durable identities made of better, stronger "stuff." That's where we are headed in the pages ahead.

Loss of identity is a lot like my son's concussion and resulting amnesia. Truth is out there, but we are separated from it. This separation leaves us feeling alone in a world full of people and gives rise to identity confusion and inner questions. *How do I find my true self? Is it up to others to define me? Is my true self within me? How can I form a strong identity that won't collapse under any life loss? What should I do when I don't know who I am?* This subconscious search leaves us emotionally and spiritually hungering in a world filled with many flavors of philosophical and psychological solutions. We can "try on" new, therapeutic versions of ourselves like we try on new clothes. Each of them is a cheap and fragile substitute for what we actually seek.

Where is the strong sense of self that is most *truly you,* and yet somehow more durable and stable than you *alone*? Where is that foundation that doesn't depend on you to try harder? Where is that identity that is unique, stable, and a "one-size-fits-*one*" solution?

Wouldn't it be nice to be able to stop trying, to finally have a durable identity, and to grow into it and enjoy it? Now that would be the best kind of *living*.

DEFINING IDENTITY

Before we proceed much further, let's define some concepts.

Your *identity* is "your deepest idea of who you are." It is "the story you tell yourself about yourself."[1] It subconsciously drives everything else in life. It is the definition of you that you have adopted—your source of value, your core trust, where you subconsciously look for meaning and validation.[2]

We all have an identity. We want and need a solid or truthful one, and we work hard to construct and secure "the one" that we believe is best. This identity causes us to think, *This is me . . . this is my fit . . .* In times of upheaval or personal loss, subconscious "who am I" questions are thrust from the backstage to the front stage of our lives—out of the shadows and into the light of examination or contemplation. We are forced to reckon with either a strong or weak identity, and whether our process for shaping it is valid or vulnerable.

Identity is not only factually "who I am," but more influentially, it is "who I *think* I am." For we all tend to believe the things we tell ourselves about ourselves. Yet "what I think about me" won't be enough. A strong identity requires objective facts, outside of myself. "What I think" will need to be validated by some external, reliable authority. This is where I will place my core trust. So, regardless, my identity will always be partially a product of what I think (internal processes) and what others say (external processes). In other words, identity is constructed both from *without* (external to you) and *within* (internal to you). And it is both a process of *discovery* and of *development*.

We always ultimately look outside of ourselves for affirmation of our identity. We are hardwired to need someone external to us—someone we value, respect, or love—to approve our identity. It must be someone we trust. Only then will the identity we seek become solidified in our psyche.

Though the term "identity" is familiar in our cultural conversation, personal identity formation takes shape as a subtext of life. Like breathing, it is an involuntary function of the soul. Is a fish aware of water? Were early humans aware of gravity? Likewise, most people are not consciously aware of their identity. Few ever pause long enough to consider how they are forming *a self*. But the fear of it falling apart or the evident anxiety when it does reveals the inherent fragility of our identities.

God calls identity the "inner being" (Eph. 3:16) and desires this part of us "to be strengthened with power through his Spirit."

When this inner "self" is weak, we feel frustrated, anxious, fearful, defeated, and unhappy. When it is strong, we feel secure, fulfilled, valuable, purposeful, and happy—at least temporarily. This is the unseen dynamic that often drives our emotions and hence our behaviors. God also refers to identity as "the heart" (Prov. 4:23) and challenges us to guard and maintain it carefully because it is connected to all other facets of life.

The subconscious "who am I?" questions always demand answers and yet are never fully, permanently satisfied with the answers our temporal, fragile world provides. For this reason, these questions are also haunting because of the intrinsic weakness of the balsa wood processes we've adopted. Past success is never enough for an unbreakable future identity, as our identity continues to demand greater success or sustained security. On the other hand, past failure demands ongoing reconstruction of a new, better identity—penance, reparations, and reinvention to compensate for the flawed self. Failed identity demands that we start over, try harder, and build better. Either way, identity built on success or failure becomes a monster we cage and feed. Eventually it eats through the cage and devours us as well.

Amidst all of this *trying* to achieve identity, we are conflicted, intuitively desiring to be more than what we do. Our core identity simply must be more than the sum of our successes or failures. We yearn to be valued for who we really are, and to fully know and realize our truest selves.

If we build with weak things, we must try feverishly to protect our creation from loss. When it collapses, we try hard to hide the shame and fake it, only to rebuild using alternate flimsy materials. In this sense, the concept of identity is either strong or weak. It motivates or demotivates us. It stabilizes or destabilizes us. It gives us either a sense of meaning or meaninglessness. A strong identity results in a positive self, while a weak identity results in a negative self. But both are deceptive in ways we will soon see.

Identity formation is the phrase we will use for how we construct or maintain our identity. It's the process we trust to define ourselves. Every waking moment, we subconsciously work to establish, maintain, or improve our identity. And everybody builds an identity from one of *three sources*. On the journey ahead, we will contrast all three—two fragile sources and one durable, trustworthy source. Growing in this third option transforms and grounds our hearts deeply and authentically.

• • •

When life hits us so hard that we lose our bearings, we are forced to turn somewhere. Do we despair, try harder, or reinvent ourselves?

What if it's simpler than all that?

Maybe you're like my son that day in my car. In your psychological and spiritual concussion, you may not know where you are or who you are, but there is a way to remember. Despite what your identity loss may look or feel like right now, there is immeasurable good to be discovered from it. Your free fall can have a soft landing and a more beautiful outcome than you could imagine. But first, you'll need to understand what's really happening within you.

Let's discover God's identity process. If you belong to Him, it will help you trust what He's doing to redefine and refine you. It will give you hope and anticipation of the new identity that He is shaping within you. If you don't yet belong to Him, understanding God's heart for you may make you want to be His child as well.

Take this identity journey with me. There's a long, winding road between where you are now and where you will ultimately feel "safe at home."

It's possible to stop trying to achieve your identity. But the journey is not what we expect.

"Trust in the Lord with all your heart, and do not lean on your own understanding. In all your ways acknowledge him, and he will make straight your paths."

PROVERBS 3:5–6

Chapter 2

SPLINTERVILLE

Facing Our Fragile Souls

"Do not let your happiness depend on
something you may lose."[1]

C. S. LEWIS, *THE FOUR LOVES*

JESUS ADDRESSED IDENTITY FORMATION. His earliest followers
experienced radical identity transformation over a short period
of time, as He predicted. Their stories are those of weak people
whose weaknesses were embarrassingly exposed. In the midst of
tragic loss, transformational events unfolded, and radical courage
materialized. The weak spontaneously became strong. The failed
and flawed quickly morphed into flourishing. Durable lives and purposeful hearts emerged from the dregs of defeat. Balsa wood identities crumbled and were rapidly replaced with rock-solid selves.

If there was hope for these first believers, there is hope for us.
What happened? How did it happen? Most importantly, can it
happen to us?

Travel with me to a seashore in Galilee about two thousand years ago. Let's examine one of history's greatest identity losses.

JESUS' FRAGILE FOLLOWERS

Jesus' followers were devastated. For three years they could taste the dream that Israel had dreamed for hundreds of years. Throughout the Scriptures, God promised redemption. He promised to deal with the nation's failures, give them new hearts, and establish them in safety and blessing forever. He promised to send them a Savior, the ultimate King they called "Messiah." And when Jesus came, there was little doubt that He was Messiah.

His claims, teachings, love, and miracles all confirmed His identity. As a result, tens of thousands of first-century people followed Jesus, and none were more devout and confident than Peter.

Peter followed Jesus, but he did so with his own out-of-sync script in mind. He launched out in his balsa wood identity, expecting Jesus to lead a nationalistic revolution, deliver Israel from Roman oppression, and establish a new kingdom. Peter was completely invested in his own idea of God's big plan, and hence his own idea of himself. This is how balsa wood identities are constructed—we shape ourselves, our world, and even God, to our own ideas. We even shape His Word to mean what we want it to mean.

We try to create ourselves rather than embracing how we are created. We write a script rather than receiving one from the Author of the story.

Toward the end of Jesus' ministry, many followers walked away because He wasn't delivering on their ideas. Trying to prepare His disciples, Jesus explained that those ideas were wrong, but many wouldn't receive or couldn't understand His explanations. They especially dismissed His teachings about Him dying or leaving.

For Peter, Splinterville (identity loss) came the night Jesus was arrested in the garden of Gethsemane. The disciples had met privately with Jesus for dinner, during which time He said some alarming things: *This is my body . . . broken for you. This is . . . my blood . . . shed for you* (see Luke 22:19–20). Ignoring this unsettling conversation, Peter and his friends later quarreled over rank and prominence in the new kingdom as they walked together. They were fighting for deck-space on their balsa wood vessels.

Their walk ended at a garden where Jesus often prayed. His demeanor was intense. With His brutal death mere hours away, Jesus began to suffer alone as His friends fell asleep. The voices of a crowd and the clanking of chains awakened them as the night came alive. Drowsy Peter was jolted by adrenaline. Earlier that night, he'd vowed to fight and defend Jesus to the death. As promised, Peter delivered a spectacular performance. He launched his weak self straight into the storm of the ages.

He leapt to his feet, grabbed his sword, and swung into action as the chief priests, the officers of the temple guard, and the elders came for Jesus. Without any directive from Jesus to defend Him, Peter swung his sword at the servant of the high priest. He missed the servant's head but lopped off his ear. With this, the scene melted into chaos—armed men readied to fight, blood flowed, and disciples prepared to pounce or flee. Defying expectations, Jesus calmed the scene, rebuked Peter, and miraculously reattached Malchus's ear. Then, unthinkably, He surrendered to the arresting officers and voluntarily went away in shackles.

The disciples were left desperately trying to anchor their weightless identities.

Wait! What just happened?

Identities shattered and disciples fled. They had invested their whole *selves* into Jesus' claims—or should we say, *their ideas* of Jesus' claims. They had staked their lives and built their hopes on their expectations of who He was, and now they were free-falling in deep loss. Everything was in question, and no anchor-point seemed reliable.

Peter followed from a distance, confused and psychologically dazed. At supper, he had said he would *never* deny Jesus, but Jesus had countered him, essentially saying, "Tonight, you will deny Me three separate times" (see John 13:37–38). A short distance from the garden, Peter waited outside the high priest's house, where Jesus was being tried. Flames danced hypnotically in the night. The rogue crowd thirsted for Jesus' blood. Peter's thoughts must have raced as the darkness of doubt and confusion enveloped him.

During these confusing hours, Peter, at three different times, vehemently denied knowing Jesus. In the distance, a rooster crowed. Then, a battered and bound Jesus crossed through a doorway a few feet away. Jesus turned toward Peter; Peter looked up. Their eyes locked, and Peter remembered Jesus' words. What he had done became crystal clear.

Splinterville.

Peter's identity was smashed against the rocks of failure. His over confident, impetuous self crumbled into an unrecognizable pile of splinters—total loss.

Jesus envisioned Peter's redemption, but Peter was clueless to what was really happening. He needed this moment if he was ever to be who God designed him to be. Weak Peter had to be lost so that strong Peter could emerge. Before Peter could have a durable identity, he needed to lose his fragile one. Jesus had foretold this to Peter, saying, "Simon, Simon, behold, Satan demanded to have you, that he might sift you like wheat, but I have prayed for you that your faith may not fail. And when you have turned again, strengthen your brothers" (Luke 22:31–32). Jesus was doing something supernatural in Peter, involving the loss of a balsa wood self and the discovery of a strong self.

Ironically, *Peter* was trying to save *Jesus*, but *Jesus* came to save *Peter*.

For the sake of understanding our own identity journeys, let's trace the "defining" of Peter in Scripture. His identity formation began as a Galilean—a poor kid in a scorned Jewish subculture. Later in life, he became a successful fisherman—providing for his family in his hometown of Capernaum, on the north shore of the Sea of Galilee. It wasn't spectacular, but it was a successful business in a beautiful place.

After Jesus' invitation to follow, Peter's identity process pivoted. He began to identify himself as a *revolutionary* and a future *cabinet leader* in Messiah's kingdom. For a couple of years, Peter's sense of self grew larger and his identity seemed strong, but deceptively so. It was self-strong—full of pride. It was artificial—strong in appearance only, and deeply fragile and ungrounded. Peter hijacked God's narrative and built his own version of self.

We tend to do the same thing.

That night outside of Jerusalem, ironically, Peter presumed he could be the savior of *the* Savior. Hours later, he was just a failure—embarrassed and humiliated. Some days later, Peter reverted back to being a Galilean fisherman again. Imagine all of these identities disintegrating in Peter's mind. After he denied Jesus and locked eyes with Him, Peter ran away and wept bitterly (Matt. 26:75).

Peter faced total brokenness. This was more than sorrow or

regret, more than confusion or fear. This collapse of self was both psychological and spiritual. Peter felt invincible, but discovered he was more vulnerable than he ever knew.

So are we.

Jesus was fulfilling a cosmic plan, while Peter was gluing together a fake self. Jesus' story for Peter was bigger and more beautiful than Peter ever imagined. But first, Peter's script had to be erased—lost.

We are privileged to witness Peter's story from afar, but Jesus desires to do the same terrifyingly wonderful work in us. He's writing a more beautiful story in our lives than we could ever imagine. But we mutiny. We hijack the story our Author is writing for us and launch our own balsa wood versions in its place. This is why it's necessary for a durable identity to begin with loss. And it's always a painful loss.

Perhaps you identify with *strong* Peter—you know who you are, and you are flourishing in confidence. Maybe you identify with *weak* Peter—you've lost your sense of self and are floundering in confusion. Peter's constructed self was both vulnerable and deceptive: his success was not durable and his failure was not final. Neither his strong nor weak self truly defined him. His strongest, truest identity hadn't yet emerged.

Neither has ours.

Successes or achievements cannot define us. Why? Because they are insufficient to give us a fullness of identity. They are temporal, fragile, and reversible. Failures and regrets cannot define us. Why? Because we are more than our failures, and those failures are subjective—based on who measures us, who we are compared to, and how we respond. If we allow failure to define us, it will crush us.

This is why loss becomes the first formational step toward a strong identity. Like Peter, we need to lose, or at least reorder, the fragile things that define us—both successes and failures. Thankfully, loss is not final or ultimate if Jesus is authoring it. It's merely the first step in a beautiful process of being made new.

DEFICIENT SOULS IN SEARCH OF IDENTITY

What do you allow to define you? Who or what gets to say who you are?

Our identity is essentially our source of three things: *acceptance, security,* and *significance. Acceptance*—who accepts me and why? What is my strongest source of affirmation? *Security*—how am I held together and "to whom or what" do I look for stability? *Significance*—what most gives me validation or a sense of value? What makes my existence meaningful? How you answer these questions is how you invisibly construct and maintain your identity.[2]

Broadly speaking, we look to four sources for acceptance, security, and significance:

- *who validates or affirms us (people)*
- *what we do well to gain that validation (performance)*
- *what we own to substantiate and secure that validation (possessions)*
- *what we desire or dream to fuel significance (purpose)*

While many of these things are subject to internal judgments, we bring them to the surface in search of external validators. We're always subconsciously asking, "Do I really matter to anyone? Am I valuable? Loved? Significant?" We seek a kind of acceptance, security, and significance we don't have to *earn* and can never *lose*, no matter what.

The inherent problem is this: we look to *temporary* things to give us *permanent* solutions. We look to others to accept us; we look to our abilities to validate us; we look to our material possessions to secure us; and we look to our personal desires or dreams to give us significance or purpose. All of these sources are breakable or changeable. People change their opinions, fail us, or abandon us—or ultimately pass away. Abilities wane or opportunities to use them are lost along with demotions or illness. Desires are fickle and can change or mislead us.

Consider how our psyches are programmed to think:

I am who affirms me. Our earliest identity comes from our family of origin and the nature and quality of loving relationships. *I am a son or daughter. I am loved or unloved. I am nurtured or neglected. I am cared for or abandoned.*

Later, these relationships morph or expand—*I am a friend, a boyfriend, a girlfriend, a single person, an adult, a fiancé, a husband, a wife, a mom, a dad, a grandparent.* The quality of love we received (or didn't) from these relationships powerfully defines either a strong or weak identity. We subconsciously rationalize: *I am loved; therefore, I am valuable.* Or, *I am not loved; therefore . . .*

This begins to show the intrinsic brokenness of the affirmation process. *If I'm loved, I have a strong sense of self. If I'm not loved, then who am I?* My sense of self is weak. Human love can give us identity, but not a *strong* one, and not a *permanent* one. Why? Because human love is often conditional, sometimes fickle, and always temporal.

For Peter, this would have included not only his nationality (as an Israelite) or his familial/village relationships in Capernaum, but also his skewed sense of Jesus' affirmation after being chosen to be a disciple. It's clear in Peter's pre-resurrection self that he had an enlarged sense of identity as a companion to Israel's long-awaited King.

I am what I do well. In early childhood we begin to form our identity based on behavior or performance that others applaud—things we are good at or things that provoke approval from others. Certain behaviors are rewarded, and others are penalized. This sends us on a lifelong quest of performance-driven identity formation. We become subtly plagued by the idea, *I am what I do. I am what I'm good at. I need others to approve of me. Performing well makes me valuable. Failing to perform makes me a failure.*

From there the road of identity formation branches out in millions of directions as I seek to discover what I do well and to fulfill the expectations of various figures in my life—parents, coaches, teachers, mentors, bosses, and role models.

In Peter's case, he could fish well. No wonder Jesus disrupted his identity with two incidents of fish-less nights, at which point Jesus nearly sank two boats with more fish than Peter had ever seen at once (Luke 5:1–10; John 21:1–11). Jesus was beginning to reveal to Peter his fragile identity—*Who am I if I'm a fisherman who can't catch fish? And who is this man who has power to fill my life with fish?*—and He desired to reveal His power to more durably and authoritatively define Peter.

Performance-based identity is powerful in all of us. If I'm athletic, I perform in sports. Winning becomes my identity source. Losing becomes my threat. If I'm artistic, I perform creatively for validation. Rejection of my art becomes my threat. We perform in many ways—from trying to win the love of another, to winning a scholarship, to attempting to win God's forgiveness through good works or religious devotion. We achieve, hoping to find a strong sense of self.

If I am what I do, then working harder becomes the *essence* of my identity, and it's driven to its ultimate edges by comparison and competition with others. If I consistently rise to or exceed the standards set by others, if I am as good as or better than others, then I enjoy a sense of strong identity. If I fail, in comparison to others or in light of others' expectations, I suffer the loss of identity. Work or achievement is not the enemy. Weak identity construction is. God created us to live fruitful lives, but He never intended that our "doing" would actually come to define us.

We intuitively know our value should not depend on our achievements. Over the course of many years, performance-based acceptance becomes psychologically exhausting as we strive to meet others' standards in order to gain a merely conditional acceptance. This flimsy conditionality hurts because we long to be loved as *beings*, not merely as *doings*—loved for who we are, not merely for what we do.

I am what I own. Consumer culture programs us for discontentment and drives us to strive for material identity. Marketers tell us it's our money, possessions, and pleasures that define us. We brand ourselves as winners, projecting a contrived self through clothing, cars, accessories, and company brands.

Material identity is weak. If I have it, I'm validated. If I lose it, I'm lost. There will always be the next style, the newest gadget, or a cooler look. Like a carrot on a stick, material success tempts me to chase a just-out-of-reach new and improved self, but never confers the "best self" it promises.

By contrast, our hearts long for real rest and contentment. We all hope to arrive someday at a destination where our needs and wants are finally fulfilled.

I am what I desire or dream. We will unpack this more later, but this identity attempts to come from within more than without. It says, *My feelings or desires reflect my deepest, truest self. My dreams define me.*

This identity search attempts a psychological deep-dive of self-discovery. It elevates individuality, shakes off external expectations, and draws us toward self-made definitions and deified emotional desires.

This identity isn't only fragile; it's volatile. Desires often change and conflict, or they can mature or grow over time. God designed us to pursue and realize big dreams and powerful purposes, but desires were never designed to own or define us.

THE WORLD'S TEMPORAL IDENTITY FACTORS

Our world imposes identity factors into our identity formation. Generally, we shape a sense of self by some combination of the following list.[3] When well-ordered in its rightful place, every one of these factors is a good gift from God. There's nothing wrong with appreciating, celebrating, cherishing, or developing these facets of our lives. But when elevated to an identity, each one fails and proves insufficient. Disordered and disproportioned identity factors become self-destructive, and all of them combined could never wholly define you.

Read this list slowly, and diagnose yourself by asking: *How much have I allowed this factor to define me?*

1. **Race/Ethnicity/Culture**—*I am my ethnicity or culture.*
   Ethnicity elevated into an identity fuels our tendencies toward racism and prejudice.

2. **Family of Origin**—*I am my familial heritage.* This reduces us to nothing more than beneficiaries or victims of our family trees.

3. **Religion/Moral Performance**—*I am a good or religious person.* This fuses our identities with systematized good behavior and imprisons us to perpetual performance.

4. **Gender**—*I am whatever gender I choose.* Gender is redefined as purely a psychological choice, shattering male/female "binaries," and forcing us to experiment with dozens of contrived options.

5. **Sexual Orientation**—*I am my sexual desires.* Lusts and physical passions reduce us to merely sexual beings.

6. **Wealth/ Possessions**—*I am my money or stuff.* Greed and materialism perpetually drive the acquiring of more to fuel our sense of self.

7. **Power/Status/Personal Capacity**—*I am my abilities.* Personal accomplishments create an insatiable drive for increased capacity and achievement.

8. **Love/Romance**—*I am my attractional qualities.* Romantic relationships become absolute and essential for feeling personal worth and acceptance.

9. **Past Abuse/Victimization**—*I am my bruises.* Wounds and past hurts can never heal because they have come to define us.

10. **Failure/Regrets**—*I am my regrets and mistakes.* Bad decisions become permanent, unforgivable, and unrecoverable regrets.

11. **Social Media/Fake Identity**—*I am my profile.* Ever-improved digital profiles promise affirmation by numbers of likes, shares, friends, or followers.

12. **Generation/Age**—*I am a Millennial, Generation X, etc.* Age and life stage elevate one generation over others.

13. **Function/Abilities**—*I am a . . . [creative, speaker, leader, etc.].* Primary abilities or roles become essential to feelings of worth and meaning.

14. **Relationships/Friendships**—*I am who accepts me.* Finding friends, fitting in, and fearing rejection become our primary drives in life.

15. **Occupation/Career**—*I am my career.* Vocational success elevated to identity will cause us to devalue people and steamroll over more valuable priorities.

16. **Personality**—*I am my temperament type.* Personality tests and descriptors (e.g., I'm an introvert, extrovert; I am funny, relatable, etc.) compartmentalize us onto spreadsheets and numbered grids to make us feel as though we understand ourselves.

Do you see how each of these things may be true (or at least partly true), meaningful, and helpful, but they can never be comprehensively defining? Each one is insufficient and can be destructively disproportioned in our identity structures. After considering these factors, we might say, *I understand that I am more than merely these things.* In fact, it might be helpful for you to read the list again, but with each factor say, *I am more than my ethnicity. I am more than my family history. I am more than . . .*

We desperately need deeper, stronger, more durable definitions.

• • •

Before we finish Peter's story, or my son Larry's, we need to discover why the world's temporal identities are so weak. Let's examine the only two identity processes the world offers and find out what these identities are actually made of.

Pretty soon, you're going to *want* to lose your weaker identity to gain a strong one.

Next stop—Magic Kingdom.

"Though the fig tree should not blossom, nor fruit be on the vines, the produce of the olive fail and the fields yield no food, the flock be cut off from the fold and there be no herd in the stalls, yet I will rejoice in the Lord; I will take joy in the God of my salvation. God, the Lord, is my strength."

HABAKKUK 3:17–19

Chapter 3

WEAK IDENTITY

Unmasking a World of Fake Selves

"They have misled my people, saying,
'Peace,' when there is no peace."

EZEKIEL 13:10

ANTICIPATION FILLED THE cool night air. Dreamy music began as I savored my last bit of sugary deliciousness that we call "cotton candy."

Lights faded. The crowd waited eagerly.

My wife and I stood motionless, arm in arm, in the middle of Main Street U.S.A. Suddenly, the world around us came alive with a series of beautiful explosions. Emotions peaked. Adrenaline surged.

Each burst accompanied perfectly synchronized music, animated scenes, and delighted gasps from nearby families. It was captivating and overwhelming to every sense. The scene repeated itself over and over with delightful force. Thunderous claps echoed. Flash, boom, then darkness. We were mesmerized.

Finally, a hypnotic calm fell over the crowd. Ethereal music played. A spotlight pierced the night and landed upon a shimmering green figure moving rapidly and erratically overhead. Green sequins. Blonde hair. Curly-toed shoes. A glowing wand.

Nearby, a child pointed up and exclaimed, "Tinker Bell!"

The crowd exploded with wonder. Young children cheered. The music soared as euphoric singers declared, "You can fly, you can fly, you can fly!"

Tinker Bell waved her wand, and leapt off the ledge of Cinderella's castle, darting across the dark sky like a laser.

The music climaxed and calmed again as a deep voice emanated from the speakers with a fatherly "happily ever after" embrace: "Grab ahold of your dreams and make them come true. For *you* are the key to unlocking your own magic. Now go. Let your dreams guide you. Reach out and find *your* Happily Ever After."[1]

It was all so dreamy. We were ready to go "make our dreams come true." It was beautiful and romantic. We hugged. We kissed. Then we tripped over the stroller next to us as park lights relit like a cup of cold water to the face. Tired, sugared-out kids cried for their beds. Visitors on motorized scooters, texting and driving, nearly rolled us over. Disney employees with long flashlights barked, "Move to the right . . . please!"

The mass exodus for the park gate brought us instantly back to the crushing reality of life on planet Earth. It was a precarious journey, navigating tired crowds, sticky hands, helium balloons, plastic light-up swords, and traffic controllers.

What happened to the happiness? Where did the magic go? What about my dreams?

Truly, fantasy and reality have a nasty, head-on collision nightly in that space. A few moments of escape come to a close with that elusive directive, "Grab ahold of your dreams and make them come true. . . . Reach out and find *your* Happily Ever After" . . . in this dog-eat-dog, survival-of-the-fittest reality.

We love it, but do we really believe it?

Admittedly, the fireworks are fun. But there's something about these fictional narratives that can reach beyond fantasy. It's partly our heart's desire for something better, and partly a culture saturated with fake messaging about how to discover "better"—but sometimes our fictional stories flow from and connect with our deeper search and our skewed perspectives on reality. Beyond the fiction, there truly are conflicting, irrational beliefs and a resulting hopelessness in our world, which essentially says, "Hope, but don't expect it to be real."

We live in a world of incoherent and deeply frustrating fake or weak identity messages.

WEAK IDENTITY NARRATIVES

There is no shortage of identity messages being forced into our hearts. In the coming pages, we will explore the messaging that is all around us—from academic institutions to pop culture, corporate America to the entertainment industry, retail marketers to automobile manufacturers. We are simply inundated with fake identity messaging and flimsy promises.

The corporate world says that market success defines us. Stephanie is a family friend—a Christian, a loving young wife and mom, a business leader, and an all-around optimistic and joyful person. She's solidly growing in good directions in every aspect of her life, but like all of us, she's navigating the tension between "who she is," "who she hopes to be," and "who others say she should be." She's wrestling with where to anchor her deepest sense of self.

Identity narratives abound around her and within her, resulting in those nagging "who am I *really*" or "who am I *now*?" questions. In studying these narratives with our church family, she emailed me expressing the real tension between her heart and her career pressures. Here's how she described it:

> Pastor Cary—in recent months and years I have dis-covered that my self-worth and identity are deeply tied to my "successes and failures." . . . This past week I have stepped down from being a sales director with [a large company]. Going from a very public leadership role back to being "just a consultant" is difficult for my ego and my heart. I am fighting the "I'm an utter failure" feeling. I am fighting the shame and embarrassment of "not making it." I am fighting asking and answering the "what's wrong with me?" question. I know in my heart that none of that matters . . . but knowing that in my heart and living that in my actions and daily thoughts is incredibly difficult at times, especially this week.

In Stephanie's case, it's not a fictional narrative, but rather the corporate narrative attempting to define her by material successes or titles. Externals are forcing their way into her psyche, demanding that she tie her sense of self to temporary things like commissions and sales numbers. It could just as easily be a more traditional narrative defining her by marital status, motherhood, or house-hold responsibilities. Neither the corporate nor the family role is bad, but neither one is comprehensively "who she is." Neither provides a durable identity, and the pressure struggles are very real—for all of us.

Academia declares that knowledge defines us. We struggle with the immense pressures of academic success and the drive to be accepted into prestigious colleges.

I live thirty minutes from Yale University, one of our nation's most prominent institutions. Rather than providing a strong identity, the academic world merely multiplies pressure, shaping a lifestyle that is unsustainable and unattainable. Just last year, the most popular class on Yale's campus was a class on "Happiness." *One-fourth* of the undergraduate student body enrolled in this elective to learn how to build a happy life. The *New York Times* quoted one freshman as saying, "In reality, a lot of us are anxious, stressed, unhappy, numb. . . . The fact that a class like this has such large interest speaks to how tired students are of numbing their emotions . . . so they can focus on their work, the next step, the next accomplishment." The article goes on to describe how today's college students are discovering that good grades, great jobs, material possessions, and all their associated pressures simply do not make us happier.[2]

Society declares that audacity and self-discovery define us. In response to discouraging racial identity narratives, African American author and activist James Baldwin wrote: "In order to survive this, you have to really dig down into yourself and re-create yourself, really, according to no image which yet exists in America. . . . You have to *decide* who you are, and force the world to deal with you, not with its *idea* of you."[3] On one hand, I want to shout, "Yes! Defy the oppression of unjust stereotypes!" But on the other, I want to say, "Wait, can *anyone* just decide who they are?" We will explore this idea later.

Pop culture says that identity is something we create—through beauty, social branding, or realized dreams. Whether it's the movie *The Greatest Showman* telling us to "live in a world that we design"[4] or Facebook giving us more than fifty gender options, our world swirls with weak identity narratives—both fictional and nonfictional. Author and theologian David Wells stated it this way: "Never before have we had more resources and technology to create a fake identity. We have the money and the social media world, and we work hard to brand ourselves, to put an image of self out there that isn't real."[5]

The sheer number of identity options available to you is overwhelming. You're standing at the edge of a field of a billion rocks, and being told that your true self is waiting under just one of them. *Where do I begin finding my true self?*

FANTASY VS. REALITY

If we look closely and think deeply, these identity messages create more questions than answers. Am I really the key to unlocking my own happiness? Can I really *make* my dreams come true? Are my aspirations truly my best guide? And does the full burden of finding my happily-ever-after rest on me alone?

What if my dreams and desires change or conflict? They're known to do that, aren't they? You want to eat healthy, but you also want to eat donuts. Both *excellent* desires in my opinion.

How do we force our best selves to materialize? With the limited control we have over life, these would have to be pretty small plans—like, "I plan to go to the pantry, and eat a Pop-Tart!"

But what about the big ones? How do we figure out which

combination of billions of options will *make* our hearts flourish? In the one-in-a-gazillion chance we guess correctly, how would we simply *will* it into reality?

It all seems so random and overwhelming. Yet, it supposedly determines our happiness and identity for the rest of our lives. The implications are so staggering, we often want to escape. It's easier not to think about it. Just grab another fistful of cotton candy and watch the fireworks.

Is it chance or fate that causes the "real me" to emerge? How do we *find ourselves* in this vast ocean of identity options? Are we doomed to experimentation, educated guesswork, hoping to get it right at some point before we die? Do we have to waste a few decades trying and failing?

What if we try relentlessly but can't find that elusive "true self"? What if we succeed and then lose it all? Worse yet, what if we succeed, and success proves unfulfilling or fragile? It's easy to find people who have everything, yet nothing. Many give a lifetime to pursue an idea of themselves that, once achieved, turns out to be unfulfilling. It's not hard to find despairing hearts in this world. Many come to believe that life itself just isn't worth living.

Weak identity structures taunt us with "go find yourself" messages like giant, cosmic bug lights. The beautiful blue is intoxicating, but the reality is dangerous. They draw us closer with dazzling promises and palpable attraction. The "happily-ever-after" message appeals to our core desires, and yet a world without a loving, personal God doesn't deliver a happily-ever-after. It doesn't even pretend to.

The logic is dangerous. Secularism in one moment says, "Go create your dream," and in another says, "You came from nothing, mean nothing, and are going to nothing." That's the ZAP! The secular narrative touches our hopes, draws us in, and then zaps us into nonexistence. It's illogical and hopeless.

How does all of this connect to our identity quest?

Whether in college classes, career seminars, motivational talks, or fairy tales, the world repeatedly tells us to look into our hearts, discover our dreams, bravely unlock the potential, and courageously make it all true. *Seize the day. Go out there and be your best you.*

Let's face it. Something about these words is both true and false. Something resonates with our hearts, and yet something else is dissonant with the reality we know. Think of those words—*dreams, heart, bravery, courage, potential.* These are noble words that awaken us to something we desire, something we once knew but seem to have lost—like a dream we can't remember.

But these are also scary words. *Wait, it's all up to me? Look inside my heart? Unlock the potential?* I gotta be honest here—I'm not that smart or powerful. Who am I kidding? The prospect of becoming the wrong me is terrifying. The possibility of trying over and over and never actually finding me is equally so.

On one hand, we want to seize life with courage and adventure. On the other, we are heavily insured, hoping to be safe from risk and loss. The paradox is paralyzing. We're looking for durable identities, and culture is telling us to *seize* them, to *make* them. We're told to be rational and strong, and then we're told that it's random fate or luck. It's a mixture of truth and deception, strength and weakness, reality and fantasy. But that bait of hopefulness leads to the trap of deep loss and despair.

One study has revealed that today's college students and young professionals are the loneliest generation in America.[6] A full 86 percent of twenty- and thirtysomething adults admit to wrestling with depression, loneliness, disappointment, and insecurity related to a "quarter-life crisis"—"a period of intense soul-searching and stress occurring in your mid 20s to early 30s, typically because you feel you're not achieving your full potential or are falling behind."[7] This crisis is a predictable season when adults realize their years of achievement aren't making them "feel" fulfilled or happy. They begin asking "what's the point of it all?" and then descend into a general despair and skepticism toward identity messages that culture has forced upon them.

In his book *The American Paradox*, David G. Myers diagnoses our nagging emptiness and despair in his subtitle: *Spiritual Hunger in an Age of Plenty*. He documents that our society overflows with material wealth and success, and yet experiences "deep spiritual poverty." We have more prosperity than ever, and yet we are more despairing than ever.[8] Hence the rise in mental illness, substance abuse, and suicide—which has increased by 33 percent in America over the past twenty years. This is largely due to increased numbers of younger Americans taking their own lives.[9] Suicide is now the second leading cause of death for Americans ages ten to thirty-four. Psychologist Jean Twenge states, "I don't think it is an exaggeration at all to say that we have a mental health crisis among adolescents in the U.S."[10]

We could note the many celebrity lives that ended in suicide: designer Kate Spade, chef Anthony Bourdain, comedian Robin Williams, and the list goes on. University of Chicago professor Allan Bloom diagnoses this generation as one whose meaning and purpose for living has been removed, resulting in general despair and disenchantment with the world.[11]

Yet, this soul emptiness is really nothing new. More than a century ago, successful Russian novelist Leo Tolstoy entered a despairing time that brought him to the verge of suicide, in spite of the fact that he was deemed to be one of the greatest writers of all time. He transparently described the identity questions that haunted him:

> I could give no reasonable meaning to any single action, or to my whole life. . . .
>
> No matter how often I may be told, "You cannot understand the meaning of life, so do not think about it, but live," I can no longer do it. . . .
>
> My question—that which at the age of fifty brought me to the verge of suicide—was the simplest of questions, lying in the soul of every man . . . it was a question without answering which one cannot live, as I had found by experience. It was: "What will come of what I'm doing today or shall do tomorrow?—What will come of my whole life?"
>
> Differently expressed, the question is: "Why should I live, why wish for anything, or do anything?" . . . "Is there any meaning in my life that the inevitable death awaiting me does not destroy?"[12]

Tolstoy, like us, couldn't just "not think about it."

The attractive bait of culture's identity messages, when swallowed, produces a soul "lostness" that is unbearable. David Wells described the modern identity search this way: "The [modern] self, therefore, has been made to bear the weight of being the center of all reality, the source of all our meaning, mystery, and morality. But all of this is asking far more than can realistically be asked. The result is that the self becomes empty and fragile."[13]

We need to look more closely at what this messaging is really doing to our hearts. We need the truth, a strong framework of unchanging reality through which to filter culture's shifting narratives.

TWO FRAGILE IDENTITY SOURCES

What should we do with this flawed messaging that is perpetually pressed into our hearts, and what is the alternative?

In 1 John 4, the aged disciple of Jesus was writing to much younger Christians, and he challenged them to be on guard—to "test the spirits" or the voices of our culture. In verse five, he stated that these anti-God voices are always speaking and being heard. He asserted, "Little children, you are from God and have overcome them, for he who is in you is greater than he who is in the world" (1 John 4:4). Earlier in the letter, he said,

> Do not love the world or the things in the world. If
> anyone loves the world, the love of the Father is not
> in him. For all that is in the world—the desires of the
> flesh and the desires of the eyes and pride of life—is not
> from the Father but is from the world. And the world is
> passing away along with its desires, but whoever does
> the will of God abides forever. (2:15–17)

The apostle John is challenging us to understand the distinction between God's reality and the world's destructive identity substitutes. Specifically, what are those substitutes? Modern philosophy identifies two primary sources of identity, and these competing identity sources show up in many of our favorite fictional stories. Philosopher Charles Taylor calls these two identities a *traditional identity* and a *modern identity*. Hold onto these terms. We will need them for rest of our journey.[14]

What is a traditional identity, and how is it fragile? What is a modern identity, and how is it fraudulent?

The road forks at this point in our journey. We could deep-dive into philosophy. That would prove laborious for all of us. I'd rather learn the same things from the stories we are all familiar with—especially those from childhood. Would you believe some of our favorite Pixar and Disney movies actually might teach us modern philosophy? Let's stand at the intersection of philosophy and familiar stories on our journey toward ultimate truth. Let's consider how these stories can help us think more deeply about the two fake identity processes.[15]

Next stop, Arendelle.

———

"Beloved, do not believe every spirit, but test the spirits to see whether they are from God, for many false prophets have gone out into the world."

1 JOHN 4:1

Chapter 4

TRADITIONAL IDENTITY

Understanding How Others Define Me

"The nail that raises its head gets pounded down."
—JAPANESE PROVERB

ELSA IS THE PRINCESS OF ARENDELLE, heir to the throne, and the wielder of some pretty freaky snow-cone powers.[1] From a child, she can whip up ice from sheer magic, which is great fun with her sister, Anna, and great conflict for Arendelle culture. Elsa's individuality is a danger to her community, and so her parents hide her. She is forbidden to use her powers for fear of the social stigma they would create.

Right on cue, Elsa and Anna lose their parents. This means they grow up reclusively hidden behind palace walls until the long-awaited coronation day when Elsa will become queen. This is her duty and destiny—to lead and serve the people of Arendelle. Pause the movie.

This is Elsa's traditional identity. It's the one she was born into. It's who she's told she must be. It's who her people expect her to be. It's what she's been prepared to become.

Hit Play on another movie. Simba just can't wait to be king, and his version of kingship will be quite different than the kingship of his father, Mufasa.[2] But after young Simba is blamed for his father's death, he flees the kingdom in shame—suffering the loss of his identity. Feeling banished and alone, he collapses in the desert—the failed king who never was. This is the loss of Simba's traditional identity. He failed at who he was supposed to be.

We could go on. Belle is expected to stay home and marry Gaston. Moana is expected to stay on her island and lead her people. Jasmine is expected to marry a powerful prince and create an international alliance. Ariel is expected to stay "under the sea" for the rest of her life.[3]

And who could ever forget *Toy Story* and the identity confusion in Buzz Lightyear, a toy who deludes himself into believing he is actually a real Space Ranger? In an epic dose of reality, his friend Woody screams into Buzz's confusion, "YOU! ARE! A! TOYYY!" To which Buzz hilariously and ironically replies, "You are a sad, strange little man. And you have my pity."[4]

This is traditional identity revealed through our favorite family narratives. I'm not trying to trivialize or juvenilize our journey, but rather trying to reveal that one of the best ways to understand secular identity formation is to study the stories we tell ourselves. Who are our heroes, and what struggles do they have? How do these and other stories teach us the concept of traditional identity?

TRADITIONAL IDENTITY—OTHERS DEFINE ME

For thousands of years, humanity has been conditioned to arrive at personal identity through our community of *others*. From ancient people groups to recent generations, people historically receive the identity into which they were born and which others defined. Quite simply, this is *who I am supposed to be* according to how others write my story.

It begins with family and then extends to tribe, village, town, and nation. Throughout most of the world today, traditional identity is the primary source of self—*I am who others say I am*. Or, *I am who you say I am*. I am defined by my ethnicity, nationality, parents, and community.

Traditional identity is external to us—forming from the outside in. We learn who we are by growing up, learning the ropes, keeping the rules, and gaining the skills to survive and succeed in the culture into which "fate" placed us.

This is all objective to us—outside of us and imposed on us. As an infant, you didn't choose your gender, ethnicity, family, name, or hometown. (You don't think I chose "Cary," do you?) You didn't choose your personality, abilities, or natural proclivities. I don't know why I hate onions; I just do. It's who I am. I don't know why I enjoy reading; I just do. It's who I am. These are the things we believe "just are" or happened to us. They are defining things that are true of us because others say so or because of "fate."

Most generations of people haven't asked, "Who am I?" because this question was answered for them. For this reason, the question is relatively new to humanity. Traditional identity is subtly imposed upon us along with the framework of cultural expectations, rules, boundaries, and behaviors that reinforce it or destroy it. *I am my* parents' child. *I am my last name. I am the heir to my father's craft. I am obligated to my family, tribe, society, religion—to be and do what others expect me to do.* We are motivated to live up to and into that identity because of the rewards.

This identity has many forms. It can be driven academically, racially, politically, economically, religiously, athletically, nationalistically, or dozens of other ways. Remember, we're looking for acceptance, security, and significance, and a traditional identity offers it, as defined by others and as we achieve their customized set of expectations.

One real-life example of traditional identity was offered in the *Atlantic* article "Workism Is Making Americans Miserable," and it begins with these words: "For the college-educated elite, work has morphed into a religious identity—promising transcendence and community, but failing to deliver." Author Derek Thompson describes that the gospel of work has replaced traditional faith, leading people into a new form of worship. He writes, "Everybody worships something. And workism is among the most potent of the new religions competing for congregants."

The article goes on to describe how workism has become the foundation of identity and purpose in our society. This is evident by the fact that we use our life margins to accomplish more work rather than rest or do other things. One of the most profound observations is that this drive is actually spiritual in nature and that our work is more than an economy—it's actually become an identity and a faith system that is proving to be insufficient. "In the past century, the American conception of work has shifted from *jobs* to *careers* to *callings*—from necessity to status to meaning."[5]

Why is workism so dangerous? It makes us feel momentarily fulfilled, and so becomes a source of identity. Achievement becomes our drug of choice, and our work then becomes a crushing god that can only produce a weak identity.

Another example of traditional identity can be found in the work of philosopher and author Jordan Peterson. Though rejecting essential biblical truth, Peterson rebukes modern adults with his treatise *12 Rules for Life*, which reads like a parental lecture on taking up responsibility, working hard, and getting your life together. It's a traditional "save yourself" message with lots of practical and workable advice, but its popularity is perplexing. A generation that rejects *ten* moral absolutes provided by a loving God apparently prefers *twelve* provided by a Canadian philosopher. His subtitle is *An Antidote to Chaos*—accurately touching the raw nerve of our longing for an identity *other* than random natural causes and meaninglessness.[6]

If you ever prided yourself in an achievement or lived up to someone else's expectations, you know a traditional identity. You worked hard to win, and others acknowledged the win, making you feel accepted, secure, and significant. Identity was validated by others because your achievement was approved—you performed well. More work or harder work was the natural result to sustain the identity process.

A traditional identity is made weak by failure—or by behavior that threatens our sense of acceptance, security, and significance. Others set the expectation, we fail to achieve, and we lose affirmation. Our sense of self is diminished, which makes life almost unbearable. We start over, try harder, work longer, or give up and run away—all to either *gain* the identity our hearts crave or *escape* the sense that we never can.

Traditional identity is a mixed bag. In many ways, it's how the world works. But in deeper ways, it's insufficient.

Let's break it down.

HOW IS TRADITIONAL IDENTITY GOOD?

Traditional identity is good because it serves the good of community and does what is noble and honorable for others.

This identity honors authority and heritage. It serves the family, the country, the church. It sacrifices itself to bless others. It lifts up civilized life with moral behavior and community ideals. It calls you to do what is best for the most people. It compels you to love sacrificially, to do what is right, regardless of your emotions or desires.

For thousands of years, traditional identity has motivated soldiers to sacrifice their lives, students to aim higher, first responders to run into harm's way, parents to provide or protect, leaders to lead well, and athletes to win. The world functions within the framework of traditional identity.

Traditional identity essentially says *you are accepted, secured, and significant as you take responsibility to live out your life for the good of others*—which is both selfless and selfish. It satisfies others' needs as well as your own. So it goes like this: *Be good and you'll have a strong self.*

Traditional identity is good as it calls you to accept your immediate community and responsibilities and to steward them for the good of a greater whole around you. This identity is why the civilized world works. It's why we pay taxes, have neighbors, and enjoy friendships. Civil and social culture works within a traditional identity framework. We all behave well for the benefit of the whole.

HOW IS TRADITIONAL IDENTITY INSUFFICIENT?

Traditional identity is insufficient because it is performance-based and conditional. A traditional identity is only as strong as you are good in the eyes of others.

Well-behaved, high-performing, and hardworking people thrive in a traditional identity world—they are rewarded for their fulfillment of responsibility. They are successful. Never mind whether they are doing what they were *created* to do. Never mind whether they are *personally fulfilled*. Acceptance, security, and significance have been achieved by hard work and good behavior. This identity is based upon your ability to increasingly do or out-do yourself for others, which is eventually unsustainable and exhausting. To use Derek Thompson's description, "The problem with this gospel—*Your dream job is out there, so never stop hustling*—is that it's a blueprint for spiritual and physical exhaustion. Long hours don't make anybody more productive or creative; they make people stressed, tired and bitter."[7]

This identity is also based upon acceptance from others when they approve of our performance, which laces our relationships with conditional factors—I am affirmed *as long as* I am producing. I am accepted *as long as* I am useful. The moment I become unproductive or un-useful, my identity is in jeopardy. The loss of acceptance, security, and significance always hangs over my head. Rejection is one failure away. And it goes both ways: do for others, and we expect them to do for us. It's a two-way street that fuels identity on both sides of the equation.

This subtly goes against our heart's desire for *unconditional* love. That desire to be loved for "who we are." We understand that marriage is loving "for better or for worse, for richer or for poorer." We instinctively expect parents to love their children unconditionally. We long for perfect, pure love—love conferred, not earned; love that is received freely, not achieved. This is love that cannot be lost by poor performance. We need to be loved in failures as much as in successes.

But traditional identity doesn't offer this kind of love. It is only as strong as your ability to meet expectations.

HOW IS TRADITIONAL IDENTITY LOSABLE?

Traditional identity is breakable and losable because it is always dependent on others. You are hopelessly hostage to outside opinions and imposed standards of measurement.

This identity cannot withstand failure and is always threatened by the possibility of shame and rejection. Fear is always hiding just below the surface. If you don't live up to the demands of others, guilt and shame will follow. Fear of rejection becomes a powerful motivator, albeit a psychologically oppressive one.

A traditional identity structure lends itself to a culture of fear, which is partially what makes powerful people powerful. They hold the power to reduce your identity—to reject, intimidate, or coerce you. Fear is the unseen foundation of many traditional identity structures. As my friend Thomas McMillan recently shared with my church family: "If you give someone the power to approve of you, you also give them the power to disapprove of you—and that is too much power to give to any individual."[8]

Personal failure can destroy a traditional identity. So can the loss of ability to perform to standard or to out-perform your past self. Traditional identity isn't only fragile and losable—it's guaranteed to be lost, later if not sooner. Why? Because nobody is perfect. You will be a disappointment to someone, and to yourself, at some point. You will hit a wall. You will break or falter. You will "pull a performance hamstring" and find out where you really stand in a world of paid producers. It's destined to fail you.

HOW IS TRADITIONAL IDENTITY CRUEL?

Traditional identity is ruthless in two ways—it is unsustainable and it steamrolls over your individuality.

In recent decades, traditional identity has been demonized for its insufficiencies. Strange? Maybe, maybe not. What could be harmful about honor and character and integrity?

There's a demon waiting in the shadows of performance-based systems. Like the scene in *Star Wars* when the garbage compactor walls begin to close in on Luke, Leia, Han, and Chewbacca, good performance closes in with demands for better and perpetual performance.[9] Over the long term, there's a price we pay with our souls. Our identities imperceptibly meld into our hard work, usually at the expense of more valuable things.

In this relentless cycle, the most valuable relationships of life (those of unconditional love) become subservient to the conditional relationships and the rewards of achievement. They must, because this is about retaining our identities. Our very core is at stake. Therefore, *we neglect those who deeply love us to please those who merely love what we produce.* Until you "can't produce," the two are extremely hard to distinguish.

Uninterrupted, this cycle leads to the loss of true relationships. We sacrifice "valuable" on the altar of "temporal" because we fear rejection. We need approval and grant others too much power over our identity.

Finally, traditional identity always subjugates *individuality* to *community. Stifle your gifts. Swallow your dreams and desires—others are depending on you.* The *others* take precedent over the *individual.*

Is this a good thing or a bad thing? Interestingly, it's both, so stay with me. Modern narratives idolize individuality, and therefore scream at the seeming injustice of community trampling it. It's almost criminalized. *Shouldn't my uniqueness and individuality matter? Shouldn't I have the right to dream, desire, and be myself?* Traditional identity says, "No. You have a responsibility to be who you *have* to be, not who you *want* to be. *Responsibility* trumps *individuality.*"

This begs the question, Must there be tension between *who I have to be* and *who I want to be*? Do individuality and community unavoidably conflict, or can there be a resolution or reconciliation between the two? Actually, it's a very prevalent false dichotomy. We'll come back to this.

FROM TRADITIONAL IDENTITY TO WHERE?

We are studying an intangible. We can't examine every possible angle, but we can learn the vocabulary and ideology to diagnose the world around us, and our own hearts. Once we see these things, we see them everywhere and never un-see them.

A significant part of our identities is built on traditional structures—which is good and normal, but also flawed and insufficient. A purely traditional identity is destined to bring us loss. It falls short and can't take us all the way home.

We all desire the approval from our people—whether family, friends, coworkers, or community. But that approval or lack of it doesn't sufficiently define us. We all need to feel accepted and significant. But those feelings are fragile and deficient. This identity is dependent on others, conditioned on good work, and dismissive of uniqueness. It is easily undone and really doesn't care about our personal dreams.

Traditional identity isn't evil; it's collapsible. It's a loss waiting to surprise us. It can't ever be the fullness of identity we need. This isn't anyone's fault; it's merely the objective reality of our world.

Elsa was conflicted about her responsibilities and her magic ice gift. Simba couldn't bear the burden of rejection at Pride Rock and responsibility for his father's death. Ariel was struggling with her father's expectations and her desire to be "where the people are." Jasmine was torn between honoring tradition and being free to marry someone she loves.

The underlying philosophies in these stories play out in our real lives as well. That's why the stories resonate with us. We feel the struggles that the characters feel in the stories we love. We identify with their identity struggles, and we cheer ourselves on in their triumphs. Why? Because in real life the definitions forced on us by others can never sufficiently define us. We are more than what we do, how we perform, or what others say we must be. And we'll never be able to live up to Peterson's twelve rules, or anybody else's rules perfectly—including our own.

As with all these examples, one indicator of a collapsing traditional identity is resentment of the structure, the people who constructed it, or those who failed to live up to it. In each of these scenarios, the characters we connect with are facing *dual struggles:* The first is the *fear* of losing a traditional identity—the fear of shame and rejection. The second is the allure of *individuality*—the passion to be true to self and personal dreams.

` • • •

If traditional identity is inherently insufficient, what are the alternatives? If the DNA of the world's way of building identity for thousands of years is this significantly flawed, what else can we do?

How do we compensate for these flaws and guard our hearts from becoming resentful and cynical toward others? How do we live for and serve others, while realizing our unique individuality, all without tying our identity to our honorable efforts? How do we avoid being hostage to the fear or intimidation of dominant people or failure?

We all need an identity that is strong, regardless of the opinions or judgments of others. Is there a way to be free, apart from sheer rebellion or defiance? And what of failure? What if my traditional identity has been smashed, like Peter's, into a pile of splinters and self-loathing?

Consider the moment Elsa embarrassingly exposes her hidden powers. Or recall the devastation when Ariel's father discovers her devilish deal with the evil sea witch Ursula. You remember that crushing scene when Buzz sees his own TV commercial and the fateful words "Not a flying toy"?[10] His final attempt to fly leaves him flattened in despair as Randy Newman soulfully sings, "I will go sailing no more."[11]

His dreams are crushed. Reality has robbed his individuality— so we might believe. Is he a stupid, insignificant toy? Or is there more to the story?

There's more to his . . . and ours as well.

"For by grace you have been saved through faith. And this is not your own doing; it is the gift of God, not a result of works, so that no one may boast."

EPHESIANS 2:8–9

Chapter 5

MODERN IDENTITY

Declaring That I Define Me

"My people have committed two evils:
they have forsaken me, the fountain of living waters,
and hewed out cisterns for themselves,
broken cisterns that can hold no water."

JEREMIAH 2:13

MY DAUGHTER, HAYLEE, and I were at the top floor of the Yale Museum of Art, where modern art—what looked to me like accidents or remnants of paint-fights—was on display.

We were quietly surrounded by artsy gawkers and security guards, one of which approached us. He sensed our confusion as we stood speechless, staring at a snow shovel hanging by fishing line. In New England, snow shovels are no unusual sight, but it seemed out of place in a prestigious art museum.

I turned to the guard and, in an appropriately hushed voice, said, "Um, maintenance left a snow shovel up here."

His serious response put a damper on my humor: "That's a work of art." He smiled with self-satisfaction.

I laughed out loud. Haylee shushed me.

"You're kidding me!"

"Nope, and it's worth a lot of money." He pointed us to the description on the wall.

Sure enough, there it was, created by French artist Marcel DuChamp in 1915. It was titled *In Advance of the Broken Arm.*

Marcel went to the 1915 equivalent of a Walmart, bought a snow shovel, hung it by fishing line, gave it a name, and called it art. The original shovel was lost—probably to a snow-covered sidewalk nearby. But Marcel's re-creations are, today, worth many thousands of dollars.

The guard continued, "I stand here all day and hear professors and classes come through. I can tell you everything about every piece of work in this gallery."

He explained that Marcel DuChamp was turning art on its head and was part of a movement called "Dadaism."[1] He was living in an era where traditional ideals had failed and fallen apart with a devastating cultural collapse called The Great War. What was prophesied to become a European Utopia before World War I descended into pointless, chaotic bloodshed and slaughter.[2]

During this traditional collapse, Marcel and his generation rose up with cynical defiance to traditional norms. Their way of peacefully protesting was through a kind of expressive, defiant art called "readymades."[3] Great art was typically defined by critics, based upon judgments of the artists' skills. With his snow shovel art, Marcel simply chose an object, hung it up, and *declared* it art. He defied standards by essentially saying, "This is art because I say so."

Call it irrational, or peaceable defiance, or resistance to traditional identity (in the art world). Whatever you call it, Marcel was not alone. Strangely, his snow shovel became incredibly valuable to the art world, not because it had intrinsic value, but because of its symbolic defiance of traditional norms. The audacity of the young artist to declare something to be art was applauded as a renegade, innovative, anti-traditional move—courageous self-discovery. Marcel revoked the world's authority to judge his art, and history has continued to unfold along this line of thinking. This leads us to the second identity process.

MODERN IDENTITY—I DEFINE ME

Culture's only alternative to traditional identity ("others define me") is what philosopher Charles Taylor calls a *modern identity*.[4] It's the life equivalent of revoking others' authority to tell me who I am. Like Marcel, modern identity breaks free and says, *I define me*. It refuses, at first, to grant the authority to externally validate the self. It rebuffs the idea that others should have jurisdiction in my life, to impose standards or expectations. It thinks, *Who are you to tell me who I am?*

The *individual* takes precedent over *others*.

At heart, a modern identity is renegade—even reckless—individualism. In its most innocent form, it seems creative, courageous, and adventurous; but in its extremes, it is irrational and self-destructive. It defines itself, disregarding the world's predefined norms and primarily God's created, authoritative definitions. It despises binaries and boundaries, regardless of their reasonableness. It prides itself on being contrary, regardless of rationale. At the root, it's a call to defy your Designer, hack your design, and experiment with alternate selves.

While traditional identity looks *outward* for a strong self, modern identity looks *inward*. It essentially says, "Look inside your inner psyche and explore who you really are, discover your *self*, and then go make it a reality—force it into being. Declare yourself to be whatever you desire."

It's the fairy tale writer in our heads—*Go make your dreams come true. Explore your options. Reject imposed identity. Reject external opinions. Make it up for yourself. Follow your heart.* All of these statements mingle truth and deception. They aren't entirely false, but they are skewed, insufficient, and dangerous. They rebel against the idea of an external authority or absolute truth.

Modern identity is a relatively new phenomenon that has gone mainstream. The entertainment industry incessantly advances the modern identity narrative. The general story line in many modern stories is: *Break free from how others define you* (traditional identity) *and construct your own definition* (modern identity). Heroes are applauded for breaking free to find themselves.

One example is Evan Hansen, a beloved Broadway character whose story resonates with the identity hunger of every human heart.[5] Early in his story, Evan sings of his social withdrawal to avoid exposure and mistakes, but he's desperately tapping on the glass of his devices, longing to be noticed, heard, and valued. He's waving through this window, wishing someone would wave back. Evan grieves the failure of his traditional identity—he doesn't fit.

He asks powerful questions that we all ask in private moments. *Who am I? Will I always be this? Will I ever be more? Will anybody ever notice me?* Listeners' hearts resonate with his search for identity. He sings that we start with stars in our eyes but eventually find that life doesn't deliver, and we ask the disappointing question, "Do I matter to anyone at all?"

In Evan's desperation for identity, he finally constructs one (modern identity) and publishes it on social media. To his great distress, it goes viral and eventually collapses in complex, heart-rending ways. Evan can't actually live up to his contrived self.

There's the irony—modern identity is fake but still demands achievement. It's built on make-believe but comes with enormous destructive pressure to live up to it.

Another example is Elsa in *Frozen*. After Elsa's public exposure, she flees to the mountains, where she defiantly delivers her popular solo "Let It Go."[6]

My favorite attraction at Disney World is—wait for it—the "Frozen Sing-Along Celebration"![7] Go ahead—you are not the first to laugh at me. What was initially my attempt to escape the heat and rest in a soft chair actually became a hilarious, entertaining experience, mostly from the performance of the four-year-old girl next to me.

At the zenith of the show, Elsa takes centerstage, the lights shift, and "snow glows white on the mountain tonight" flows mysteriously from her kingdom of isolation (modern identity). Delightfully, from the moment Elsa appeared, the little girl to my left was channeling her in full costume and with perfect synchronization.

The room echoed energetically as Elsa loudly proclaimed her independence and let it all go. The room was alive. Dads plugged their ears. Music roared. Children cheered. And the little girl next to me fully performed with Elsa until she finally, defiantly stomped and stared, declaring that "the cold never bothered [her] anyway."

With the last thunderous thud, snow began to fall, and the little girl stood on her chair, spread her arms wide toward the stage, and proclaimed at the top of her little lungs, "I AM ELSAAAAAA!"

It's great fun, but there is more than entertainment in the actual message. It's complex philosophy playing out in family entertainment and revealing the real tension of our psyches. Let's consider a few dynamics of the modern identity woven into these narratives.

First, this is the essence of modern identity—cast off everything and everybody that holds you back. Defy. Set yourself free. Let it go and stop caring what anybody says. It's utterly self-centered, reactionary, and bent on self-fulfillment, no matter who gets crushed.

Second, it sounds adventurous, audacious, and attractive, but it's fake. Therefore, it is impotent—powerless to ever fulfill us. In the movie, defiant Elsa ends up isolated, alone, and empty. She *does* care and she isn't happy being alone. In fact, when her trip into modern identity fails, she needs her family and her people, and she reconciles valuable relationships. She ends up being the good queen of—you guessed it—Arendelle!

The "let it go" message always eventually leads back to "run back home, you need your people!" The call of self-discovery leads to isolation and eventually a desperate hope for reconciliation. Our hearts weren't designed to bear the burden of self-definition, and sheer rebellion will only ultimately isolate you and leave you miserable and longing for home.

This problematic philosophy unfolds within three concepts of God. The first is secular godlessness—*There is no God, no creator, no purpose, no meaning, and you are nothing more than randomly evolved, biological matter. Therefore, your desire for identity is fake, so make up fake meaning and fake significance.*

The second is the god of moralistic, therapeutic deism: *a concierge who serves you or an impersonal, intangible force to be leveraged. Define and improve yourself through oneness with the universe and help from spirit guides.*

The third is the defiance of God—*It's my life. I can do whatever I want, and nobody can tell me otherwise.*

Once you see the modern identity message, you see it everywhere, from entertainment to self-help books to high school guidance counselors. People are desperate to discover themselves, and we celebrate stories where the lead character experiences this discovery.

In *Beauty and the Beast,* Belle sings that she wants more than the provincial plans of others. She wants adventure and independence—not bad things in themselves. The call, though, is not merely to dream or pursue adventure, but to cast away traditional identity and to roll over those standing in the way. In *The Little Mermaid,* Ariel longs to break free from the water to live on the land. In *Aladdin,* Jasmine is told of a whole new world where no one can obstruct her search for love. *Moana* feels the call of the water and sings that no one knows how far it goes.

These narratives, though fun and fictional, reveal the soul tensions we all feel in desiring to be our "true selves." Real-world modern identity narratives are equally pervasive.

REAL-WORLD MODERN IDENTITY NARRATIVES

Pastor and writer Eugene Park stated that we live in "a world where people are weighed down and exhausted by various cross-pressures: to perform, to be accepted, to become gods of our own making, to define (and constantly redefine) ourselves in expressive and novel ways."[8]

Pastor Tim Keller describes the modern identity this way:

> In the past every culture assumed that you found truth outside the self, either in God or tradition or some transcendent values, or in the good of your family and community. That meant we had some objective, external norms by which disputes between persons could be adjudicated. Now our culture says we find truth inside ourselves; we are told to "live our truth" and never sacrifice our happiness and inner desires for someone else. To do so is unhealthy at best—oppression at worst.[9]

The idea of being "gods of our own making" or finding "truth inside ourselves" sounds ludicrous to an objective mind, but this is the actual messaging of our world. Once you grasp the modern identity message, you can't miss it. It's mainstream, and this generation is profoundly shaped by it. Let's consider some recent examples:

Modern identity can be mystical. In 2019, *Time* magazine published the article "Yes, Witches Are Real. I Know Because I Am One." Author Pam Grossman provides an example of a modern identity narrative. She describes being a witch as both literal and figurative and explains to female readers that being a witch is an identity that readers can assume. She explains the need for female readers to defy traditional norms in favor of individualistic identities.

Raised in a traditional Jewish home, Grossman eventually sought out individualized and mystical belief systems like paganism. This is how the modern identity rejects authority (especially God's ultimate authority) in favor of autonomy and lesser, more controllable and shapeable "god-forces." She describes self-proclaimed witches as a "society of people who fight from the fringes for the liberty to be our weirdest and most wondrous selves" and declares that a witch is essentially a self-liberated, "independent operator."[10]

Modern identity can be sexual. The modern sexual narrative, including Facebook's multiplicity of gender options, defines you by your physical desires or personal preferences. The modern identity liberates you from God's or anyone else's predetermined definitions, sending you into an endless expanse of self-reinvention and experimentation.

Author and Yale professor Josh Knobe has written about a new term—experimental philosophy—"finding your true self" by testing various philosophies. In 2011, he wrote a piece for the *New York Times* titled "In Search of the True Self," in which he describes one man's sexual struggle and various philosophical ways to arrive at the "true self." He profiles the modern identity when he writes:

> We might tell him that what he really needs to do is just look deep within and be true to himself. Indeed, this advice has become a ubiquitous refrain. It can be found in high art and literature (Polonius's "To thine own self be true"), in catchy pop songs (Madonna's "Express Yourself") and in endless advertisements for self-help programs and yoga retreats ("Unlock your soul; become your authentic self"). It is, perhaps, one of the distinctive ideals of modern life.[11]

He describes the philosophical struggle that the modern identity message creates. How do we discern which aspects of our person, personality, or being actually constitute the truest self? Is the real you found in the desires you suppress? Or is the true self found in suppressing fleeting desires for a more substantive core reality? He provides no concrete solutions, but accurately expresses our present modern crisis of the soul—how do we go about defining or discovering our true selves as the modern identity demands?

These modern narratives are endless. If you have ever resented traditional definitions and considered breaking free to be yourself, you understand the essence of modern identity. It essentially says: *Tradition is holding you hostage. Your only hope is to hear your heart and define yourself.* Traditional identity's flaws make this modern alternative attractive, but modern identity can never be what it promises. It touches a raw nerve but then drops us into lies, anger, and despair.

Let's take a closer look.

HOW DOES MODERN IDENTITY APPEAR TO BE GOOD?

Modern identity attempts to value individuality. It's a promising alternative to traditional identity's suppression of individuality, which essentially says, *Desires are dangerous, selfish, and misleading. Kill or stifle them.* Modern identity attempts to salvage uniqueness. When traditional structures say *conform*, modern identity says, *Wait, that's not who you really are.* Because of this, modern identity appears to validate personal desires or dreams. It seems to give place to the *you-shaped* qualities that make you a one and only.

The tension over desires and individuality is real in all of us. On one hand, unbridled individualism is destructive, but this is an incomplete view. On the other hand, individuality is God's idea. He created uniqueness and gives place to good desires and dreams. Joseph dreamed of saving his family. David dreamed of building God's temple. Abram dreamed for a son. Peter dreamed for Messiah. Paul dreamed to preach the gospel in Rome. God created the heart to dream, and He realizes our unique design: "Delight yourself in the LORD, and he will give you the desires of your heart" (Ps. 37:4) and "May he grant you your heart's desire and fulfill all your plans!" (Ps. 20:4).

HOW IS MODERN IDENTITY INSUFFICIENT?

Modern identity is irrational. In a strange twist of lunacy, it commands *self* to define itself—which is implausible. Modern identity destroys or downsizes God. Why? Because *you* are the supreme authority, and God must be tamed to fit within your sovereignty. This is reminiscent of William Ernest Henley's poem "Invictus," in which he defies death, declaring: "I am the master of my fate, I am the captain of my soul."[12]

In the absence of an authoritative creator, we can write our own version of truth, craft our own stories, and command our own destinies, but what small destinies they become. A destiny I can control and a god I can shape must be *smaller* than me. This means I live a small destiny with a small god that can't help me with my biggest problems or questions.

Modern identity isn't real because it begins with the premise that there is no such thing as "real"—there is only "your version of real" and "my version of real," and both die with us.

HOW IS MODERN IDENTITY FRAGILE?

Modern identity dangerously elevates individuality. It is all *promise* and no *product*. It can't deliver a strong identity. It merely taunts us to escape traditionalism, offering up a vending machine solution— *Just be whoever you want to be.*

Modern identity enthrones individuality. It makes uniqueness the supreme lord of your life. *Trust your heart since you can't trust God, and you can't trust others. Only you can fulfill you.*

Good things are taken to bad places in this narrative. Uniqueness, individuality, giftedness, personal dreams, and feelings are elevated to the place of defining you, directing you. Consider for a moment the soul-crushing burden of *you* having to accurately discover, define, and fulfill your *self*.

Suddenly, passions drag you through life on a leash. They own you, and this self-proclaimed freedom becomes slavery. You now serve your insatiable desires. When deified, the gifts of individuality become reckless taskmasters driving you but never actually fulfilling you. Dare I say, *you* could never love you the way *God* does.

Who hasn't seen the human heart shift, without warning, from desiring one romance to another, one career to another, one dream to another. Emotions are fluid. With hearts at the helm, we become ships without rudders, lost at sea, driven wherever the winds of passion take us.

If nothing else, our dreams mature with age, wisdom, and experience—they grow up and take on new forms and ideals. Additionally, fulfilled selfish desires lose their fulfillment as time passes, giving way to greater desires for more, newer, and better. Desires are wonderful gifts but terrible guides, and they are powerless to define my true self.

HOW IS MODERN IDENTITY CRUEL?

Modern identity is cruel in two ways. First, it never settles—it always requires a new, improved, better self. Modern identity demands that I discover or invent *The One-and-Only-Me*, in my own mind. It requires that I distinguish myself from the crowd. It says, *Be the anti-norm.* In some, it is quietly subversive, determined to subtly choose an opposing path, and other times it is audacious and defiantly demands attention. This places enormous pressure on our psyches to shatter norms and create exceptions—alternate versions of our self.

Second, this identity produces massive anxiety. Imagine being thrown far into the deep end of the ocean, commanded to find a lost dime that fell from a cruise ship. The "be whoever you want to be" ideology casts you into an endless ocean of options looking for ten cents' worth of self. It leaves you there to swim alone for life. It applauds your audacity and crushes you with impossibility at the same time.

DANGEROUS IDENTITIES

Before we move forward, let's summarize the six dangers of the traditional and modern identities:

Danger #1: Disguised Identity

Modern identity is a disguised traditional identity. "Finding yourself" is a process *imposed* by others that still demands external validation *from others*. If you go into your heart and decide your snow shovel is art, like DuChamp, you still won't be validated until others agree with you, "Yes, that's art!"

Danger #2: Raging Identity

Affirmation from others is never enough, and ultimately gives way to anger. These identities unavoidably look to others to validate us in ways that they can't. It's a precursor to *everybody* failing you. The identity demands are contradictory—*Humanity, please validate me. But, you're just human, and have no right to judge!* It's a complex mind game that ends in anger.

Danger #3: Conflicted Identity

The tension between community and individuality is false. The conflict between "who we *have* to be" and "who we *want* to be" is wonderfully resolvable. The world gives us a menu of two weak options—a rule-keeping (traditional) identity or a rule-breaking (modern) identity. Rule-keeping earns us a false sense of loving community and conditional acceptance. A rule-breaking identity allows us to be an Avenger but isolates us in fantasy and fake affirmation (i.e., "Okay, you're Captain America!"). We are forced to choose between two flawed options. It's like asking me if I want pizza with onions or a turkey sandwich with onions. I want the option without onions. Where is the identity without weakness?

Danger #4: Horizontal Identity

Weak identities never give true vertical validation. If *others* define you or *you* define you, then your definition is *horizontal*. We're looking in the wrong direction. Strong identity is *vertical*—found by looking upward. It must come *externally*, but it cannot come *horizontally*.

Danger #5: Wounded Identity

Weak identity imprisons us to the pains of our past. Past pain can *refine* us, but can never *define* us. We are more than "victims" or "abused." Greater purpose and higher love must overshadow the horizontal hurt inflicted. Your scars may define your journey, but they do not define *you*. They actually bear no impact upon your truest definition or value in your Creator's eyes.

Danger #6: Mistaken Identity

Religion reduces Jesus to merely an alternate version of a traditional identity. It reduces the Bible to a book of rules and reduces Jesus to a good example to emulate. Religion gives us new behaviors and hard work, by which we either construct a traditional identity or alternately hide in fear and failure. In contrast, the gospel of Jesus offers us new selves, overcoming both weak identities with a strong *third alternative*, which we will soon discover.

To summarize, a traditional identity tells me *I am who others expect me to be*. A modern identity tells me *I am who I say I am*. Both objectify, depersonalize, reduce, and burden me with the impossible hard work of self-salvation. If they were works of art, both a traditional and a modern identity could appropriately be titled "In Advance of the Broken Life."

These are the only two identities offered to us by our world. Either we will be who others say we must be, or we will be whoever we want to be. We live up to others' demands or to our own. We work hard for others or work hard for ourselves. It's a simple "*you define me or I define me*" either-or proposition. Thankfully there's a third, and far superior, option.

Both weak identities have elements of attraction. Both are flawed. Both leave us empty and asking, "Who am I, *really*?" And both leave us ping-ponging between the *individual* and the *others* as they tug against each other. It's a good recipe for identity vertigo and despair.

• • •

We crave individual identity but long for transcendent value and purpose. Individuality and community. Uniqueness and transcendence. Do the two meet? Can they reconcile and become friends? If so, how?

This is me—broken, failed, and needy. Can anybody come to the rescue and redeem me? Can anybody define me accurately, comprehensively, or authoritatively? Can anybody give me value and love I can't lose and a self that can't sink in this fragile world?

We aren't longing for horizontal identity. We are longing for a *vertical* identity. Stop looking outward. Stop looking inward. Better identity materials have been made available at great cost. The apostle Peter is about to find out. We will too.

Let's stop losing and start finding.

"Come to me, all who labor and are heavy laden, and I will give you rest. Take my yoke upon you, and learn from me, for I am gentle and lowly in heart, and you will find rest for your souls."

MATTHEW 11:28–29

TRADITIONAL VERSUS MODERN IDENTITY

This chart contrasts the two weak identities and provides a summary that clarifies the depth of their differences.

Traditional Identity	Modern Identity
Others define me	I define me
I am what I do	I am what I desire
Who I am supposed to be	Who I want to be
Be who others say	Be who I say
Value community	Value individuality
Looks outward	Looks inward
Begins outside, works in	Begins inside, works out
Live responsibly	Live adventurously
Pursue duty	Pursue dreams
External validation	Internal validation
Seeking affirmation	Demanding affirmation
Performance-driven	Desire-driven
Substantive	Mystical
Hard work/effort	Self-discovery/reinvention
Others focused	Self-focused
Sacrificial, honorable	Greedy, demanding
Lose myself to others	Lose myself to me
Altruistic	Individualistic
Fit in	Stand out
Be usual	Be exceptional
Achieve your *self*	Discover your *self*

Traditional Identity	Modern Identity
Construct your *self*	Create your *self*
Follow directions	Follow dreams
Keep the rules	Break the rules
Reinforce the rules	Run from the rules
Comply to the system	Create your own system
Live up to standards	Live out of personal passions
Do what is noble	Do what feels good

Part Two

FINDING

"How much happier you would be, how much more of you there would be, if the hammer of a higher God could smash your small cosmos...."[1]
—G. K. CHESTERTON

OSWALD CHAMBERS called God's identity process "breaking the husk of my individual independence of God, and the emancipation of my personality into oneness with Himself, not for my own ideas, but for absolute loyalty to Jesus."[2]

Losing leads to finding. Surrendering my fragile self to Jesus makes finding a strong self wonderfully inevitable. Until I am free from self-definition, I cannot discover His ultimate definition. We resign our *selves* to Jesus and discover a lifetime of adventure in who He is, who He calls us, and why He created us. The question that Chambers poses is this—"Is He going to help Himself to us, or are we taken up with our conception of what we are going to be?"[3]

Bring your weak identity, with all of its brokenness and insuffi-
ciency, to Him. Entrust your *self* and your story to Him.

Here's how He writes a new, beautiful, fulfilling story.

Chapter 6

LOSING TO FIND

Encountering Jesus' Radical Invitation

"For whoever would save his life will lose it,
but whoever loses his life for my sake
and the gospel's will save it."

MARK 8:35

THE FIRST PALE GLOW of morning light crept its way over the eastern hills above the Sea of Galilee. It had been another long night of failure, in a long string of failures that began that devastating night Jesus was arrested. Days had passed since Jesus' resurrection, but Peter was frustrated, fatigued, and floating in his empty fishing vessel. He was a failed disciple, a failed revolutionary, a failed loyalist, and even now, a failed fisherman. He couldn't get *anything* right. You can almost see him kicking the side of the boat, miserably muttering under his breath all night long. He was tired and agitated, his fish-less nets cruel reminders of his long string of letdowns. He was a living catastrophe. His soul was as empty as his boat.

He was drifting and had no place to land. He'd lost every dream he dared to dream, and likely had no idea how to answer the question, "Who am I *now*?" He needed sleep after the long, fruitless night. His emotions swung wildly, traipsing through a sludge of devastated memories. Three years of dreams gone, time wasted. And fishing failed to get his mind off of it.

The elation of Jesus' resurrection was overshadowed by Peter's assumption that he would be an outcast. After his failures, he believed he had no place with Jesus. His identity likely floundered. With self-loathing, he may have told himself, "I'm no leader. I'm no soldier or revolutionary. I'm not even a decent *fisherman*."

As the first full rays of sun topped the high eastern ridges, he noticed a distant, haze-shrouded figure on the shoreline. Lazy wisps of smoke danced upward from a flickering morning fire. The faint smell of flame-cooked fish reminded Peter how hungry he was.

Another memory flash—that time when Jesus . . . No. He wouldn't let his mind go there again. "The irony, though—that guy on the shore is *cooking fish* and I've been fishing all night for *nothing*."

Peter's life was as empty as his nets. His identity structures and formation processes had failed. I'm like Peter. Are you? A bit of success sprinkled over a boatload of failure. Have you been expelled from early life dreams, part by providence and part by choice, tempted to stand, numb, staring at your brokenness, asking "Why?" and "Now, who am I?"

Identity loss feels like a huge step backward, but actually, it is God's first step forward. It seems like nothing but a pile of letdowns and questions.

But Jesus is grilling fish on the seashore, just a couple hundred yards away.

• • •

In the wake of losing his wife to cancer, C. S. Lewis wrote in *A Grief Observed*:

> God has not been trying an experiment on my faith or love in order to find out their quality. He knew it already. It was I who didn't. In this trial He makes us occupy the dock, the witness box, and the bench all at once. He always knew that my temple was a house of cards. His only way of making me realize the fact was to knock it down.[1]

What if God permits the collapse of our houses of cards—our weak selves—only so He can build something more real and durable? What if identity loss is His way of saving us from deeper, eternal loss? Loss, in God's economy, is not the end; it's the beginning. He saves us from what most oppresses us to give us what we most desire.

How is this true? How does Jesus permit identity loss, and why is it necessary? Since we've seen that horizontal identities are fragile, wouldn't it be gracious for God to deliver us and give us durable selves? And since that deliverance is painful and disorienting, doesn't it make sense that He would prepare us for it and walk with us through it as only a loving Father could?

JESUS' RADICAL IDENTITY OFFER

Jesus taught on identity, and Peter was there to hear. On more than one occasion, Jesus said, "For whoever would *save his life* will lose it, but whoever *loses his life* for my sake will save it" (Luke 9:24). In Luke 14:26, He similarly said that His disciples would be required to "hate" their own lives.

Obviously, Jesus isn't telling us to hate living. He's warning us to hate the weak ways we construct our selves. How does He say this? The New Testament uses three different Greek words for our word *life*—each with distinct meaning.

The first is *bios*[2]—our physical existence and physiology.

The second is *zoe*[3]—fullness of life, a lifetime, or the life breathed into man by God as a living soul. *Zoe* life is God's life—the abundant life that Jesus promised in John 10:10.

Finally, the word Jesus used for *life* in each of these teachings (and more) is *psuche*[4]—one's inner self. Our modern English equivalent is *psyche*—the deepest part of our rational being, our identity.

Jesus is calling His followers to lose their psyche to Him. In essence, He's saying, "Lose your identity—your constructed self—and you will find your created self—your true identity. Lose your balsa wood self, and let Me give you a seaworthy self. Lose who you think you are, lose who you tell yourself you're supposed to be, lose who others expect you to be, and I will transform you into who you *really* are. Attempt to define your own identity, and you will never really find it. Lose your identity to Me and the gospel, and you will find the solid identity you most desire."

Jesus is proposing a full surrender or deconstruction of the identities we've studied. He's describing an abandonment of our dependence on traditional and modern ideas for our core definitions. He calls out traditional and modern identities as frauds, and He invites us to lose our fragile psyches for something fulfilling and enduring.

He invites us into a relationship of losing and finding—deconstruction and reconstruction. At first this seems terrifying—like a flying leap off a psychological cliff. Abandon the self you or others have constructed? Lose the psyche you cultivate and protect? Surrender your right to define yourself? Yes! This is the point where our fears are raised, and our "little faith" is exposed (Matt. 6:30).

This is asking too much, we think. We would rather add a little bit of God to our fragile selves to modify them and make them better. We prefer for God to improve us, not make us new—a much more invasive process. We never imagined such a comprehensive and disruptive reordering of our core selves. This is the place where we begin to argue the good aspects of the identity we've built "for God" and how He would never require us to abandon such well-constructed work. Surely, He's thinking, "Well done!"

Lose my *self* to what? To whom? He says, *for my sake and the gospel's.* It's an intentional surrender to Jesus. The word He uses for "saving your psyche" describes deliverance, protection, healing, wholeness, and safety. He is offering something wonderful—a new, stronger, more durable and fulfilling sense of self. He's offering a superior alternative to the traditional and modern identities; but giving up our tightly held psychological securities proves difficult and painful.

The implication of Jesus' statement is both profound and extravagant. He is offering a new, third identity alternative—a new psyche that He has redeemed and reconstructed. This is not an identity *you* can construct, but rather one He creates. It cannot be *achieved* in your own strength, but it can be *received* because of what Jesus did for you. But the experience of this new self is preceded by loss. His first prescribed step to having a solid identity is that we must yield up the fragile selves that we've nurtured.

The gospel of Jesus doesn't only offer you a place in heaven. It brings you into a relationship with God that *remakes* the most sinful, broken, and fragile part of who you are. It is not merely a door you step through once, but rather an ocean you swim in every day. The gospel re-creates you, and experiencing it at your core is a redefining experience. It's a new identity in which you stand, daily, for the rest of your life—"I would remind you, brothers, of the gospel I preached to you, which you received, in which you stand" (1 Cor. 15:1).

Jesus looks you in the face and says, "Trust Me to remove all of your anchor points, so I can give you a true, strong, permanent foundation."

Can you bear the thought? Could you trust Him that much?

Truth is, you can't be found until you've first been lost.

UNAVOIDABLE LOSS

The high, midday sun meant the well would be deserted.[5] Few retrieved water in the midday heat, and the woman preferred to go alone to avoid the social awkwardness. Life had not been kind to this strong-minded woman. She was getting by—surviving—but her heart had long been crushed. Her once youthful ideals and dreams were lost—smashed on the rocks of betrayal, abandonment, and rejection. As she walked alone, she stifled these thoughts, trying to starve hope and focus on survival: *Just get through another day. You don't need love, you need water.*

Her traditional Samaritan culture gave her few rights and little acknowledgment as an individual. It is entirely possible that she'd been married, used, and abandoned by five different husbands. In her culture, they were possibly husbands only in the *legal* sense— marriages of societal convenience and patriarchal dominance— generally oppressive and exploitative to the role of women.

Her heart had likely been trampled, her identity crushed, and her soul emaciated by one abandonment after another. Had she ever known true love? Her culture wasn't one that would have acknowledged her as a soul of value. Perhaps she'd been used and disowned so many times, she didn't really know who she was.

Her traditional culture gave her no authority to initiate divorce, and no legitimate say in who she married. She was an object to use and discard. Once she proved unuseful—either by husbands who lusted after others or by a womb that was unable to give them children—she was cast aside. First-century divorce was both rampant and frivolous.

Her search gave way to her sin. Her patriarchal culture left her destitute unless she could find masculine provision or protection; and the less she was valued, the more willing she was to compromise. Either the man that presently gave her safe harbor would not marry her, or she was willing to sin for the sake of survival. Either way, it was no life. It was a living death. It gave no value or validation. It objectified and depersonalized, but it was at least *survival*—a place to live, food to eat. It was a way to get by in a world designed to trample and shame failed people like her.

The dust stirred with each laborious step toward the well. How many hundreds of midday trips had she made? How many times had she conversed with herself about her emptiness, her failures, the husbands that left her (or that she had left), and the life she once dreamed of? I imagine her inner conversation: "Will I ever be loved or lovable? Is there any hope for recovery from my failed past? Why won't he marry me? Why won't someone see me, love me, cherish me for who I am?" Her hard life strengthened her survival-hardened exterior, but also left the wounds of her heart vulnerable and her guilt palpable.

Her thoughts were interrupted as the distant well came into view. A man was sitting there. In part, she thought, *He's a man and will likely not speak to me.* That thought strengthened as she drew closer and realized that He was also Jewish. It was strange to see a Jew in Samaria, but she was relieved to think, *There's no way he will speak to me, being a woman and a Samaritan.*

As she approached the well, she tried to avoid eye contact, but couldn't help but notice that the traveler's kind face was unashamedly looking in her direction. Obviously winded and weary from His journey, He was catching His breath and making no effort to avoid her presence. Feeling His uncharacteristically cordial stare, she finally stopped and looked Him squarely in the eyes. She was wounded, but not timid.

He smiled warmly. "Would you mind giving me a drink of water?"

"Seriously? You're a Jew and I'm a woman *and* a Samaritan, and You want me to give You water? Don't you know Jews hate Samaritans?"

Jesus' smile broadened again, perhaps with a slight laugh, like a parent on Christmas morning anticipating the giving of some fabulous gift. "If you knew the gift God has for you . . . if you knew who I am, you would ask Me for living water and I would give it to you" (see John 4:10).

She didn't understand the game He seemed to be playing, but she certainly had the fortitude to play along. She replied, "You're sitting here thirsty with no rope or bucket—no way to get water from this well—asking me for a drink, but offering me miracle water. Where do You get that 'living water' from? Who do You think You are, anyway?" (see vv. 11–12).

Jesus took the conversation precisely where He wanted it. He walked into Samaria on purpose. He came to this well specifically to meet this woman, in spite of her ethnicity and past. He valued her, loved her, validated her, and held a beautiful, redeemed future for her. Every detail played out precisely according to His will. Right on cue, she asked Him who He was. His response turned the conversation from physical to spiritual. He lovingly pointed out weak, insufficient solutions to soul thirsts, and offered this wounded woman something she had stopped hoping for—water of life for her soul.

"This well merely gives physical water—you drink it and before long you're thirsty again. But I can give you a kind of water that will ultimately and permanently fulfill all of your thirsts."

What a strange claim. This time her tone is curious, if not puzzled. "Sir, give me this water—I would love to never thirst or come to draw water from this well again" (see v. 15). She's still thinking physical thirsts. He's thinking spiritual thirsts.

Then Jesus compassionately but pointedly drove straight at her heart. "Go get your husband and come back..." (see v. 16). It would have been typical for men to deal with men, but that's not what Jesus was doing. He was peeling back the hard exterior to expose her sin as well as her wounded heart. He was exposing her failures and her losses—not to torment or traumatize her, but to redeem and heal her. Ultimately, He was revealing Himself as the solution to her soul thirst, and inviting her to repent and receive His grace.

I wonder if she felt a twinge of emotion at the word "husband." Maybe she wanted one but didn't have one. Or, perhaps she was "done" with husbands. We don't know, but her response was brief: "I don't have a husband" (see v. 17).

She was utterly exposed before this complete stranger. She expected him to be so many things—disdainful, prejudiced, racial, dismissive, even scoffing. But he wasn't. This man was vastly different from any she had known.

It was the most contemptible thing a woman in a first-century traditional culture could be or say. She was alone, unloved, abandoned, useless. She tried to appear numb to the condition, but it was always there because it had resulted in such a long history of sinful decisions. Likely, there was a ubiquitous, self-condemning narrative in her psyche—*I am rejected and I've failed. God doesn't want me and neither does anybody else.* In traditional identity cultures, if you *have* no one, you *are* no one.

Traditional cultures were not (and are not) kind to women, but Jesus was and is. Traditional identity is not kind to outcasts or failures. But Jesus is. Jesus shattered every social, cultural, religious, traditional, and racial norm to reach this woman. The gospel not only elevates women, but it esteems and values every one of us in beautiful, God-conferred, unconditional love and grace—regardless of how wounded, sinful, or rejected we are.

Jesus' response is revelatory, not accusatory: "You're right. No husband. Five of them have come and gone, and the man in your life now isn't your husband." He isn't condemning her; He's exposing her thirst so He can quench it.

Five husbands—He knows! I'm not a wife, just a concubine—He knows! I'm a failure and a Samaritan, He's a Jewish prophet—He cares ... about me ... for me ... in spite of me. I can imagine her thoughts racing as the surface conversation scrambled toward cultural theology, but her heart conversation dove inward toward love, forgiveness, and redemption—and ultimately toward Messiah, the One who promised to resolve all of the brokenness of her world.

Imagine the hope that leapt into her reality with breathtaking delight when these words came from Jesus' lips ...

"Yes—Messiah. That's who I am, and I'm sitting here talking to *you*!" He must have smiled.

I'm not trying to be irreverent, but I sort of picture Him standing up, waving His arms and saying, "Ta-da! Here I am. In the flesh. Just for you. All the way in Samaria, in the heat, in love. You matter! You are valuable! You mean the world to Me and I came here right now to tell you—I and *only* I can save you and take you home forever! I'm the husband you've always wanted, the Savior you've waited for, the God you've worshiped, and the hope you've tried to bury. Dig it up and dust it off—because I know who you are, why you are, where you are! Hope is *Me*, and I'm here for *you*!" Little did she know, He was not only there to transform her, but also to use her to bring many Samaritans to similar trust in Jesus. She had no idea she was about to become the first missionary to Samaria!

This is in essence what God said in Isaiah 54:5–6, "Your Maker is your husband, the LORD of hosts is his name; and the Holy One of Israel is your Redeemer, the God of the whole earth he is called. For the LORD has called you like a wife deserted and grieved in spirit, like a wife of youth when she is cast off, says your God."

I apologize for all the exclamation points . . . but what love!

I have an idea that Jesus couldn't wait to say this to her. Everything in the conversation led to that one statement, and every failure of her past, every wound of her heart or question of her identity, was resolved in it. Her whole life had built toward, moved toward, and culminated in that one single moment.

Jesus is Messiah. He came into Samaria in the midday heat to find me. He knows me and loves me. He values, understands, and validates me. He speaks to me, invites me, and cares about me. He offers me something no one else can give.

Jesus meets us in our loss and utterly transforms it forever.

Her losing led to finding. So can yours.

. . .

We need healthy identities. But we struggle with insufficient and sinful ones. Through all of our identity formation, we are weak beings pretending to be strong, vulnerable beings pretending to be invincible, worried beings pretending to be certain, sinful beings pretending to be good, insecure beings pretending to be confident, messy beings pretending to be clean, broken beings pretending to be whole, fearful beings pretending to be courageous.

For all of our hard work to project strong selves, we either succeed, knowing that it's temporal and pretend, or we fail, knowing that every restart is leading to another dead end. We attempt to construct something that is truly beyond our reach.

We are always one "stiff wind" or, like Peter, one night of failure, away from total loss—the collapse of our weak identity. As Jesus said, apart from Him, whatever identity we construct (for good or bad) will always be ultimately lost.

Jesus' teaching is preventative and redemptive. His warning is not merely fatalistic nihilism. It is an optimistic, hopeful alternative. He is compassionately calling us to reckon with the reality we hide from. We hide behind fake strength, hard work, achievement, and insurance policies. But He breaks through and lovingly brings us face-to-face with our spiritualized, psychological "house of cards."

Think practically about it: Youth or beauty is one decade away from loss. Career is one job-loss or economic crash away from loss. Strength and ability are one tragedy or diagnosis away from loss. A relationship is one heartbeat or rejection away from loss. A desires-driven identity is one conflicting passion away from loss. The same sorts of things could be said for every identity factor we've studied.

Wherever you anchor your heart, that is where you are vulnerable. That is where loss becomes inevitable.

Late in the writing of this book, the world has literally been shut down by an unprecedented pandemic. A single, microscopic organism caused every "certain thing" to come into question. All over the globe, the bottom has fallen out from under our feet. Nations and people are dealing with unparalleled anxiety and uncertainty— health, safety, economy, and social stability have all come into question. These events have wreaked havoc on our souls with the sudden sense of loss or potential loss. Fear and despair have peaked as the inherent instability of life has been thrust front and center in our psyches. Rarely has the world collectively experienced such deep loss related to a single event. Nearly everybody on the planet has recently become acutely aware of the fragility of their core identity.

Enter Jesus' invitation to find in Him "living water"—a true, durable source of *psuche*. In light of weaker options, Jesus' offer requires serious consideration. He made possible the *only safe loss* and the *only strong self.*

Safe loss can be entered willingly, knowing it will lead to finding something greater. Safe loss is based on love and trust. Safe loss is a dad standing in a swimming pool, inviting his four-year-old son to jump into his arms. It is that moment you fall, but you fall into a safer, more secure place than you've ever been before. It's when you finally relinquish control, only to discover Someone more powerful, more loving, and more generous is actually at the helm of your heart, and you are safe in His hands.

Jesus' identity invitation sums up like this: *Lose your deepest psyche (your soul) to My good news, and let Me make you new. Let Me provide your truest, strongest self. Lose to Me what you're going to lose regardless, and let Me replace it with that which you can never find on your own, and which you can never lose again!*

THE UNFOLDING PROCESS OF LOSING AND FINDING

Oswald Chambers wrote: "God can never make us wine if we object to the fingers He uses to crush us with."[6] That crushing season—the space between losing your identity and finding it in the gospel—is precarious. It's a time when despair and doubt are always looking over your shoulder. Jesus promises eventual flourishing, but in our loss, we can't see it and wonder if we will ever experience it. We feel like He has failed us. We read Scriptures like, "The righteous flourish like the palm tree. . . . They are planted in the house of the LORD; they flourish in the courts of our God" (Ps. 92:12–13). We want that flourishing identity, but it seems a million miles from where we are.

During a season of loss, if you let Him, Jesus will begin to teach you the essence of a gospel identity. His gospel offers us an inner *something* that is resilient, no matter what other identity factors are lost. He grows a flourishing identity in a floundering culture. But it cost Him everything.

Losing your self to Jesus is temporarily painful, but not nearly as painful as His loss for you.

It's time we get back to that man grilling fish on the shoreline. Like the Samaritan woman, for Peter, for me, for you—Everything is about to change.

"I will betroth you to me forever. I will betroth you
to me in righteousness and in justice,
in steadfast love and in mercy. I will betroth you
to me in faithfulness. And you shall know the LORD."

HOSEA 2:19–20

Chapter 7

JESUS' LOSS

Falling Apart at the Foot of a Cross

"I have prayed for thee, that thy faith fail not:
and when thou art converted,
strengthen thy brethren."

JESUS TO PETER, LUKE 22:32 (KJV)

"HAVE YOU GUYS CAUGHT ANYTHING?" The voice echoed off the lake, but Peter was lost in his own frustration, oblivious to its familiar tone.

"No," they shouted back, embarrassed and a bit annoyed by the spectator onshore.

"If you guys throw that net over the right side of the ship, you'll find fish."

Who does this guy think he is? Likely in a fatigued, "whatever" stupor, they tossed the net overboard one more time. Suddenly, the boat surged sideways. The men scrambled for balance. The net tightened. Adrenaline rushed. Instantly the net filled with large fish—153 to be exact. A déjà vu moment. Eyes widened as memories flashed back nearly three years—this is exactly what had happened when Jesus first called Peter (Luke 5).

Resurrected Jesus came to Galilee to draw Peter back to where it all began. *Remember, Peter. Remember who I said you would be. Follow Me. Come after Me and fish for men.*

"It's Jesus!" John pointed to the guy onshore.

Strangely, and without thinking, Peter put on his cloak, irrationally dove into the water, and swam for shore. The cool waters of Galilee flowed across Peter's face, mingling indistinguishably with the tears. A mixture of joy and fear simultaneously flooded his bottomed-out psyche. He didn't know what to do or say. He only knew that Jesus came to him—*for him* . . . maybe.

Peter was numb to his own identity, but he knew who Jesus was—and as each thrust of his arms pulled him closer to the shoreline, his heart dared to hope again. *Does Jesus want me back? Is the dream somehow still alive? Is there redemption for me, after all?*

Seconds later, Peter sloshed his way out of the water, hesitating. Awkward. *What now?*

Jesus broke the stifling silence. "Bring the fish you caught up here by the fire. I made you guys some breakfast. Come and eat" (see John 21:9–12).

For men, food is an easy distraction from failure. So, with little hesitation, these displaced followers of Jesus huddled around a morning fire—and one by one, Jesus handed them warm bread and grilled fish. Imagine this moment.

He was dead. Now He was alive. It was real. This was no hallucination or fantasy—no ghostly appearance. This was Jesus in the flesh. The crucifixion was not failure; it was destined. Jesus died voluntarily. He went to Jerusalem to die. He had to lose Himself for Peter, so that Peter could ultimately and eternally be found.

God calls this redemption, and He wants it to happen to you too. The resurrection of Jesus redefined everything for those who believed in Jesus. Prior to this moment, Peter was anything *but* a success. After this moment, success was conferred upon him in permanent, indestructible ways.

Come close to the fire. Sense the palpable failure in the psyches of Jesus' disciples. Smell the wood smoke and fish. Feel the Galilean morning sunshine. Smell the naturally sweet Galilean breeze. See the compassion and quiet resolve in Jesus' countenance. Consider how precisely and personally He planned this moment. Hear His heart and loving words as He graciously redefined these failures.

Acceptance. He served them. His hands stretched forth to one man at a time with warm bread and fresh fish. They can't help but notice the nail scars. They can't help but remember how they failed Him. He loves them. He accepts them—but certainly not on their own merit.

Security. He provided for them. They failed at fishing. They couldn't provide for their own families or pay their own bills, yet He filled their nets with 153 large fish—a precise number likely for a precise need not mentioned in the story.

Significance. He called them back into His purpose. They had given up on Him, disappointed that He wasn't writing the story they'd hoped for. But He hasn't given up on them. He's just getting started. They are finally at rock bottom. They've lost themselves, and this is where His best work begins, so long as they lose *to Him*. They need Him in their loss. It all needs to fall into His hands.

His resurrection revealed He's writing a bigger story, and now He invites them back into it.

It was the moment the broken man feared—the confrontation

he avoided. This was the tongue-lashing he deserved. He blew it and he knew it. Everybody did. And Peter was sure this was his public shaming—the moment he would hear, "It's over. I've replaced you with someone reliable."

Perhaps the others were glad He addressed Peter.

"Simon, son of John, do you love me more than these?" (John 21:15). Jesus' tone was warm, His scarred hand likely gesturing toward the fish and Peter's friends—a metaphor for Peter's flawed and flattened identity. (Why else would Jesus want that large net of fish brought to the fireside?)

Maybe it's elliptical—maybe He's asking Peter if he loves Him more than the others love Him. Either way, it's a probing question. Jesus' followers probably disliked when He asked questions because He already knew the answers. Jesus never asked a question for information. His questions were always rhetorical—His way of bringing them (and us) face-to-face with realities we are willfully avoiding. (Omniscience can be annoying at times.) Isn't it amazing that He knows every thought we think, but loves us still?

"Yes, Lord; you know that I love you." Peter is embarrassed that his actions say otherwise. *Here it comes. This is where He's going to berate and reject me.*

"Feed my lambs."

Wait, what?

Again, and then again a third time, the same question is asked, the same answer is given, and the same invitation is extended. I can see Jesus lean in, look into his eyes, and slowly repeat Himself: "Feed. My. Sheep."

RECONSTRUCTED

In this poignant moment, Jesus began to reconstruct Peter's identity. He invited him forward from failure and conferred upon him a stronger, more significant self than Peter ever imagined. Think again of the identity structures of *acceptance, security,* and *significance*:

Peter deserved to be rejected. But Jesus *accepted* him.

Peter's failure brought insecurity. But Jesus *secured* him.

Peter's inner self is lost. But Jesus offered him new *significance*.

Acceptance. Security. Significance—provided by crucified, resurrected Jesus. This was the God-man visiting earth, the Creator of the universe, having conquered death, declaring Peter accepted, secured, and significant. This was authoritative, loving validation that was equally unconditional and unlosable.

This was an act of grace and love offered freely to Peter, though he deserved the opposite. The Creator invited Peter back into the story of the ages—accepted, forgiven, secured, and called forward in profound purpose after utter loss and failure. Peter did nothing to deserve or achieve this. It was not based on his effort. Jesus did the work.

This is the good news that Jesus brought to humanity. *You can't save yourself—I will do it. You can't reinvent yourself—I will re-create you. You can't secure yourself—I will secure you.* He died to make it possible.

Peter will never be the same after this moment, and neither will you when this process unfolds. It isn't until you lose *who you think you are* that Jesus can reveal *who you really are.*

This is what God calls *salvation* and *sanctification*. *Salvation* takes place in a moment of belief or faith. *Sanctification* is a biblical word for the deconstruction and reconstruction process, how God graciously and patiently transforms us for the duration of our lives.

Death precedes life. Losing precedes finding. Failure precedes success. It's counterintuitive—a paradox. It goes against everything life teaches us. It smacks against other identity structures. Everyone and everything in life says, "Live up to . . ." But Jesus says, "Stop trying. Lose your *self*, your efforts, your hard work. Lose your fragile ways of saving yourself. Stop pretending."

Both traditional and modern identities say that "salvation" is up to you. Religion says God is attracted to your virtue. Morality says God is attracted to your goodness. Performance-based systems teach that you are accepted by your efforts and acceptability (emphasis on *ability*.) *Get your act together. Be better. Improve yourself. Earn your validation. Build your own identity.*

Jesus steps forward and says, "God is attracted to your weakness" (2 Cor. 12:9). He is drawn to human emptiness, humility, and authenticity. He exposes us in order to call us to repentance so He can forgive and fully embrace us. Throughout our lives, He cultivates us through deep loss so we might be forever found.

JESUS LOST HIMSELF—FOR YOU

Jesus doesn't only prepare us and walk with us through the loss of self; He first lost Himself for us. He has been there and back—for *you*.

The story of the Bible is a single plotline that points to Jesus and the gospel story. From the first page of Genesis to the last page of Revelation, the Bible is God's story of redemptive history—what God has done and is doing in history to redeem us, bring us back to Himself, and remake us. And throughout the story, like every story, there is a growing tension.

In *The Lord of the Rings*, the tension lies in the question of how a weakling Hobbit will overcome the powers of darkness to place an evil ring into a volcanic mountain to save Middle-earth.[1] In *Star Wars*, the tension builds as we ask how the dark Empire will be defeated by an unlikely Jedi.[2] Every good plot has a growing tension that must be resolved: How will the prince defeat the dragon that has captured the princess? How will wrong be made right? How will evil be defeated and right prevail?

Likewise, the narrative of Scripture develops a growing tension: How will God redeem the rebellion and death that has devastated creation? More personally, how will God redeem what's wrong with me and give me a way back to Himself? How can God give me a new self?

The great unfolding tension resides between God's love on one hand and His holiness on the other. To the reader it seems that God's perfection (His holiness) will demand justice and judgment on all sin, in which case we would justly fall under His condemnation. We are all guilty before Him. (See Rom. 3:10, 23.)

Yet, God also reveals Himself as loving. He promises to redeem, forgive, rescue, and restore what is wrong. He promises salvation—a way back to Him and a way to avoid His judgment. He promises to give us new hearts. (See Ezek. 36:25–26.) So, in seemingly contradictory ways, His holiness demands justice, but His love demands forgiveness. The real tension in the plot is the question of how God will satisfy both His holiness and His love. Justice demands payment for sin, but love promises rescue and forgiveness—and if God compromises on either, He would be something less than perfect.[3]

In fact, to save us, He must be *both* holy and loving. He must find a way to execute perfect justice and express perfect love at the same time. In regards to me, He must find a way to judge my sin and rescue my soul at the same time—this is what holiness and love require. One promise can't win over the other. They must both be satisfied and fulfilled, or He would be something less than the God He reveals Himself to be.

Jesus' death on the cross is the ultimate resolution to this tension. He forever fulfilled God's holy demands by living the perfect life that we can't live—He fulfilled all expectations. Then, on the cross, He absorbed God's judgment and wrath for our sins while simultaneously displaying God's perfect, sacrificial love for us. The cross of Jesus is the pinnacle moment of human history, where Jesus lost His life to reclaim us. Holiness was fulfilled. Love was poured out. It turns out God is both holy and loving, but to fully display that holy love and to give us a way back to Him, He had to come personally to earth to suffer and die in our place.

On the cross, Jesus destroyed any myth of reason or religion that says we can save ourselves or define ourselves. On the cross He opened the arms of God, inviting all of humanity to run freely back into the extravagant love of our Father and to find new life and new selves in relationship with Him.

The cross was humanity's worst poured out upon God's best so that God's best could forever be poured out upon believing humanity. This leads to a remarkable consideration: it cost Jesus everything to rescue you. He doesn't ask you to lose your life to Him without credibility—He first suffered loss for you.

He experienced loss to win you and to bring you into eternity with Himself. "The joy set before Him" mentioned in Hebrews 12:2 was not only your redemption as His valuable treasure, but also the restoration of all of creation and His ultimate glorification as eternal King, preeminent over all things forever (Col. 1:12–20). To personalize it, you were what made the loss *worth it* to Jesus. He lost His life (*psuche*) to redeem yours and make a *new you* (John 10:11).

When He cried from the cross, "My God, my God, why have you forsaken me?" (Matt. 27:46), He suffered ultimate loss so that we would never have to. He bore our brokenness and fragility. He became our sin and poured out God's perfect wrath and justice upon that sinfulness through His sacrificial death. He was our substitute in the war on death. His blood for our life. His life lost; ours saved. He sacrificed Himself for our failures so that He could confer all His goodness upon us unconditionally.

Through His death, He absorbed your failures so that through His resurrection He could give you His perfect life and love. In so doing, He proved that losing yourself to Him is not only safe, it's reasonable and desirable. He proved His love for you. He proved He is trustworthy. He proved He has your best interest at heart as your ultimate source of authoritative validation. He proved that *only with Him* are you unconditionally and eternally *safe*.

You can trust Him with your loss.

In Mark 10:45, Jesus made this statement about Himself: "For even the Son of Man came . . . to give his life a ransom for many." You guessed it. *Psuche*. He came to lose His psyche so you could find yours. Jesus doesn't simply say, "Go jump off of a psychological cliff into My care." *He first did it for you.* He leapt into the jaws of death to release you and bring you home.

Later, Paul described Jesus' loss in this way: "Jesus, who, though he was in the form of God, did not count equality with God a thing to be grasped, but emptied himself, by taking the form of a servant, being born in the likeness of men. And being found in human form, he humbled himself by becoming obedient to the point of death, even death on a cross" (Phil. 2:5–8).

Jesus' loss was an act of humiliating service, culminating in His voluntary death on a cross, so that through this gospel He could make us who we were *always meant to be*.

The reason we construct weak, horizontal identities is that our sin and separation from God have left us with no other option. Without the gospel, we can't look to our Creator for acceptance because we've been banished from Him, and therefore we have been banished from our true selves. But for the cross of Jesus, we would be left with only horizontal, fake options—*others define me, I define me*.

For Jesus' followers, the miracle of His death and resurrection drove His redefining love from head to heart and truly transformed them. Tim Keller states it this way: "The gospel is this: We are more sinful and flawed in ourselves than we ever dared believe, yet at the very same time we are more loved and accepted in Jesus Christ than we ever dared hope."[4]

Jesus called this "new birth" and "everlasting life" in John 3:3 and 3:16. He said in John 5:24 that our belief in Him causes us to pass from death to life. In John 10:10, He said He had come to give *abundant* life. All of these references are *"zoe* life"—an unlosable, indestructible fullness of life that only God can provide. It only comes vertically through Jesus.

Jesus lost His *psuche* to give you *zoe*—His full life in exchange for your fractured life. He lost Himself in a horizontal world to resurrect you into vertical love and the very life of God. This salvation generates a new psyche within you. This is profoundly good news.

• • •

It was in the days after Jesus' loss that the scene on the seashore of Galilee unfolded. Jesus was alive, and His resurrection changed everything—and everyone who believed it. Jesus brought life from death. He predicted Peter's loss (Luke 22:31–32) and then met him at the seashore with warm bread, smoked fish, and a boatload of grace.

The lives of Jesus' followers changed radically that day. They were redefined. He is doing the same redefining work in you. Your loss is not final, and your story is still unfolding. Jesus is writing a *new script*, and you're going to love it!

Loss is painful. But loss of traditional and modern identities is also liberating. To be free from weaker identities is to be ready to grow in grace and truth. Because of Jesus, the third identity option is finally accessible.

Enter, gospel identity . . .

"Whatever it will cost you to be with God is nothing compared to what it cost Him to be with you."[5]

TIM KELLER

Chapter 8

GOSPEL IDENTITY

Celebrating How Jesus Defines Me

"Therefore, if anyone is in Christ, he is a new creation.
The old has passed away; behold, the new has come."

2 CORINTHIANS 5:17

THE ROAD BEFORE US slithered downhill out of the mountains of
Southern California. My son was struggling in the seat next to
me. Our ski trip turned into a medical emergency—a concussion
resulting in memory loss—and sent Larry into a panic attack. He
was in a psychological free fall, having lost most of his reference
points, and his emotions were scrambling for solid ground.

At this point, all kidding was off the table. The look in his eyes
dramatically raised my level of alarm. Despite his panic, he kept
using the name *Dad*. That's when it hit me. *He knows me; he trusts me.*

As I pulled the car over, I turned toward him from the driver's
seat. I placed my hands on his shoulders and issued a firm command. "Larry, look at me! Look into my eyes. Take a breath."

He did.

I continued, slowly. "Larry, do you know *who I am*?" I punctuated each word as if it were the most important question I'd ever asked.

"Yes. You're Dad," he said.

I watched his face calm. "Yes, Larry. I am Dad. I know who you are, where we are, why we're here. I know how we got here and how to get you home."

His breathing slowed. His eyes locked onto mine. Tears brimmed over the rims of his eyes. Fear began to dissipate. He was trying hard to remember, to no avail.

"Keep looking at me and listen carefully. I am Dad. Do you know that?"

He nodded.

"I am Dad, and I know who you are, where we are, and where we're going." The repetition of those truths quieted him further. "Right now, your brain is bruised and needs to rest from remembering. Don't panic. I've got you. I'm not going anywhere, and I'm going to get you home. Do you understand?"

With every breath, Larry's troubled mind found a place to rest in his father. He accepted my definitions. He rested in the fact that he knew me and *I knew him*. Moments later, he asked, "Dad, will my memories come back?" His fear began to build again. "What if they don't? What if I'm never able to remember again?"

I repeated the routine. Over and over I reminded Larry: "I'm Dad, and I know who you are. We are going home. I'll drive. Stop trying. Just rest. I'm with you."

Larry experienced deep loss. Everything he knew about himself had been mangled by the accident. He couldn't patch it together because he couldn't even find the pieces. As he sat in fear and uncertainty, what he most needed was the assurance of his *true identity*—the knowledge of who he *really* was, given by an authority who loved him and actually knew the truth. He needed reliable orientation to the world around him—the kind that would resolve his noisy, internal chaos.

He couldn't make up his own answers, and he couldn't trust the contrived answers of a stranger. The combination of truth and love had to be in the driver's seat of Larry's mind.

Enter Dad!

It was my authoritative love that grounded him and rescued him from his unreliable imagination. My knowledge liberated him from trying to remember. He received the identity I conferred upon him.

Similarly, truth and love must be in the driver's seat of our psyches. If we remove the truthful, loving, personal God from His place, we remain hopelessly lost in chaos and floundering to secure our *selves* with fragile solutions or meaningless rules of survival. Anything less than the authoritative validation of a loving Father leaves us victim to weak identities.

Wouldn't you like an identity that never fails from a Father whose love never fails?

Enter Jesus.

GOSPEL IDENTITY—JESUS DEFINES ME

To understand the redefining nature of what Jesus has done through the gospel, I need to tell you a story about where the word *gospel* came from. It's a word that not only means *you're saved*, it also means *you're made new and free to flourish in a new kind of life.*

Let's make a short trip to ancient Greece. You'll see what I mean. Possibly a mixture of truth and legend, the story goes like this:

It was 490 BC, and the Athenians were terrified. The Persian

Empire was sailing toward Greece with orders from King Darius I to march into Athens and burn it to the ground. It was to be a bloody and merciless slaughter—a ruthless territorial expansion that would permanently redefine Greece and the world.

The city of Athens mobilized a woefully insufficient army of citizens, unable to convince the neighboring Spartans to come to their defense. The Athenians had long believed they were helpless without Sparta and that the powerful Persians simply couldn't be defeated. They prepared for the worst as the Athenian army, along with soldiers from nearby Plataea, left home, expecting to never return. Wives and children wept as their husbands and fathers marched off to battle at the Aegean coast. For days, the situation seemed hopeless as the Athenians waited in fear, expecting to see the Persian army marching toward their defenseless city.

As expected, the Persians landed at the city of Marathon, but the Grecians managed to place the battle in a strategic location prior to the landing. Contrary to expectations, Athens's forces pressed into the battle, outsmarted their enemies, and sent the Persian army running toward their ships. The Greeks overtook them and brought a huge victory for their families and nation.

As they celebrated in Marathon, they remembered their families and friends at home, who remained terrified. It was a strangely polarized situation—celebration in Marathon and suspended horror in Athens—with no way to quickly get the good news back home.

Though he had already fought the battle of his life, a soldier was summoned immediately and given the task of running the good news twenty-six miles, from Marathon back to Athens. He was to publicly herald the victory. I imagine new life surged into his battle-weary body, and energizing adrenaline coursed through his veins as his new mission drove him on.

The Athenians must have held their breath, seeing a lone runner returning to their city. *What kind of news does he carry? Is the battle lost or won? Will he warn us to flee or announce our deliverance?* And what emotion must have erupted in the city as his cries of victory echoed ahead of him. The city celebrated, and the Athenian people were transformed because of this battle. The victory elevated Athens to prominence in Grecian culture, proved the Persians could be defeated, and showed the Athenians they could successfully defend themselves without the Spartans. This redefining moment produced two hundred years of flourishing Greek culture, not to mention a lot of happy wives and children.[1] Runners still run "marathons" of twenty-six miles, commemorating the victory to this day.

The Greeks had a term for the runner who heralded good news and its rewards. The word is *euaggelion*—the same word the New Testament uses for the gospel. The word expresses the public heralding and rewards of a victorious battle. This is the word picture God gives us to describe the gospel.[2]

If the Greeks had lost the battle, the runner would have made the trek, but with a terrifying message: "The battle is lost. The Persians are coming. Run for your lives, or fight for your lives! Save yourselves!" In essence, weak identities give us bad news: *The battle is lost; run for your life or fight for your life! Save yourself! It's up to you.* Religion, philosophy, and self-help ideologies all amount to the bad news of how to save yourself.

Weak identities flow from bad news—*What you must do for yourself.* A gospel identity flows from good news—*What Jesus did for you.*

Jesus is both the conquering hero and the heralding runner shouting good news into your heart. *You are loved, secure, and significant. Follow Me and I will make you . . .*

EXPERIENCING GOSPEL LOVE

The essence of a gospel identity grows as we immerse our hearts into what Jesus has done for us. We can *know* about it without actually *experiencing* it, but it's the *experience* that transforms us. It has to sink from our heads to our hearts, like the news of the runner would have for the citizens of Athens. It's when we understand that Jesus is far better than we dreamed, and His plans are far more wonderful than our scripts. He's a very big Savior who won a very big battle calling us into His very big love and purpose.

Jesus broke into time and space to rescue us, a conquering hero riding into battle to fight for those He loves. He defeated death, secured victory, and ascended out of battle as a valiant prince. (See Eph. 4:8–9.) He promises the gift of full and everlasting life to all who entrust themselves to Him. It erupts within us the moment we truly comprehend it. This is when we stop telling our Creator who we are and start accepting His victorious love to define us. This is, at our core, to be rooted and grounded in Jesus as our supreme, defining authority (Col. 2:7).

This is *who I really am based on who He really is.*

This is to fully rely on how Jesus defines me. In choosing Him, I lose autonomy to define myself, but I gain everything my heart is seeking.

The gospel makes your eyes go up and your heart go deep. Your identity goes vertical. You rest in ultimate reality—*I belong to God, and He has given me all of Himself.* You grasp the soul-redefining statement, "If God is for us, who can be against us?" (Rom. 8:31).

You don't live up to others' demands or your own. Jesus already did that for you. You don't strive to be who others say you must be or who you want to be, but you're finally free to be who God designed you to be. You don't live to please others or yourself because God finds pleasure in you through Jesus—and living in and out of His pleasure is the most defining and joyfully motivating experience in life.

GOSPEL IDENTITY VS. OTHER IDENTITIES

Traditional identity gives priority to the *others* and modern identity gives priority to the *individual*, but a gospel identity gives priority to *Jesus*—and He gives value to *both*! Jesus brings the dichotomy together and reconciles the conflict between *community* and *individuality*. The two come together in ways that resolve our hearts, fulfill our lives, connect us with our God, and strategically position us in the lives of those He calls us to love.

This is where individual uniqueness meets transcendent value and purpose in ways that both fulfill your heart and your call to bless others. It's the meeting point of all of the attractional qualities of traditional and modern identities without any of the flaws or fragility.

The gospel grounds you in vertical value and graces you with horizontal purpose. The vertical relationship you have with Jesus becomes your supply of fullness, which then overflows horizontally in loving service of others. It affirms God-given individuality, properly realizing your uniqueness and properly restraining it at the same time. It also affirms the value of community, responsibility, and purely motivated love without enslaving you to people's opinions or systems. It is radically fulfilling on every level.

It doesn't crush individuality, and it doesn't feel the need to run from community. It's full and satisfied in both spaces together. It grants you security and stability, and also prevents arrogance, dishonor, or defiance. It motivates you to serve in love, to labor from acceptance (because you *are* accepted, not so that you *will be*), and to honor God and others from a humble heart of gratitude.

A gospel identity is free from fear and motivated *by* love *to* love. This way of living is peaceful, energizing, and life-giving as opposed to anxious and depleting and feverishly working.

Welcome to the new you! This is who you were created to be.

Traditional identity says, "Obey out of duty." Modern identity says, "Disobey in liberty." Gospel identity says, "You are loved, so respond in loving obedience." (See John 14:15; 15:10.) Traditional identity says, "Stifle your dreams and desires for the sake of others." Modern identity says, "Express your dreams despite others." Gospel identity says, "Follow Jesus, the fulfillment of better dreams that will move you to love others." (See John 13:34.)

Being shaped by the gospel will require the rest of your life. This is why Paul said we can live confidently in the fact that Jesus began a good work in us and will continue that work until we see Him (Phil. 1:6). First Jesus is *born* in you (John 3:16), and then the identity and character of Jesus is *formed* in you—"My little children, for whom I am again in the anguish of childbirth until Christ is formed in you!" (Gal. 4:19).

In essence, we don't need to find our true selves, follow our hearts, or chase traditional and modern identity lies. We need to experience *being found* by our Father. He alone knows who we really are.

THERE'S NOTHING LIKE BEING FOUND

"Dad, are you sure?" Larry's eyes revealed the calm that had returned to his mind. He was asking me if I was *sure* his memory would return.

"Yes, Larry, I am absolutely sure."

Through the entire ordeal, Larry never questioned who I was. His own sense of self was smashed, but his reference points in me (Dad) remained. This is how a gospel identity grounds you regardless of life circumstances.

He let out a sigh, slowly put his head back, and lowered his seat. His breathing slowed, and his imagination calmed. I would guess he was thinking, *I don't know who I am, but my dad does.* Resting in my assurance gave him peace even before the crisis was resolved. He closed his eyes and drifted to sleep.

I drove the winding mountain pass deep in thought. *How often have I feared or worried my way through life, trying to figure out who I am or who I'm supposed to be when I need to simply rest and let the truth about who Jesus is sink in. I need to accept what He has done for me and is doing in me. In Him my inner world can have calm and strength.*

This time it was *me* who sighed and prayed for Larry and myself. *Jesus, please heal him, and please heal me in the same way.* I slowly navigated each turn, not wanting to jostle my son's bruised brain. His healing took time, but his sense of security was regained. Miles later, we ascended into the High Desert, and journeyed safely home.

It took more than a year for Larry's brain to heal. He struggled with headaches, memory loss, and focus. School classes were more difficult, and memorizing for tests was nearly impossible. He faced much frustration that year, but he never questioned who he was.

My words grounded Larry that day the same way God's Word grounds me. Lies and imagination became powerless. Anxiety expired as Larry embraced truth and rested in his father's love. This is how the gospel works in our psyche. The more we understand and appropriate it, the more it puts every identity struggle to rest.

Have you surrendered your psyche to Jesus' declaration of good news? Have you accepted who He says you are? Nothing else can so permanently transform your heart in all the ways that define you and make you free.

GOSPEL IDENTITY FREES US

Jesus came to make us free from *other people* and free to be accepted by God once again. In terms of identity, the gospel makes you flourish in a world of traditional structures without being dominated by them. Jesus grants you a higher definition. In Him, you are free to grow into His image, not your own or someone else's. When your highest allegiance is Jesus, He will motivate you to love others without seeking an identity from them.

Jesus also came to make us free from *ourselves* and from being lost in an ocean of self-definition. In terms of identity, the gospel affirms your individuality and makes your unique design significant to God and valuable to others.

Gospel identity gives us in reality what other options promise and can't deliver. This is the version of us that cannot be *constructed*; it was *created*. We cannot work to *win* it; Jesus did the work to *redeem* it. We cannot live *up* to it; we must learn to live *out* of it.

The gospel shapes us as givers rather than takers. We approach relationships from fullness rather than emptiness. We approach life from provision rather than neediness. We pour ourselves out in all the loving and honorable ways a traditional identity would demand, but willingly and gladly, and not for identity, but from it. We can serve lovingly regardless of the response from others. Our core motivation and core definition goes vertical. All insecurities melt into His full security.

This approach thinks this way: *I am the child of a limitless, loving Father. He has welcomed me into His heart, and placed me strategi-*

cally into His purposes. He created me to be who I am, where I am, for those He placed in my life. I can confidently be who He designed and calls me. I can run my own race without comparing, contending, winning over others, or living to please others. I can serve others without needing their validation. I can live in obscurity—yet completely fulfilled—if that is my Father's call. He gives me the value my heart desires. Loving Him leads to obeying. Being defined by Him leads to peace of heart. Being known and cared for by Him produces deep joy and security that allows me to love others freely.

Good news! You don't have to go searching for yourself. He knows you. He's found you. It's His voice you most need to hear, not your own, your heart's, or your spirit guide's. Your Creator and Definer has authored the truest version of you.

If by chance you have never turned to Him in faith and welcomed Him into your heart—why not right now? It's a simple moment of belief (John 3:16) and expressed faith (Rom. 10:9–10, 13). Call out to Jesus personally and ask Him to come into your life right now, as Savior and Lord. Let your identity journey with Jesus begin by receiving the forgiveness and love He died to provide.

He knows who you really are! Put your head back. Sigh with contentment, not defeat. Rest. He knows you, and He's bringing you home.

JESUS, OPEN OUR EYES

After living for more than twenty years in the desert, I had forgotten fireflies. Then, unexpectedly, they returned to my life. Shortly after our relocation to New England, I stood on my back deck one summer night when a faint flicker transported me back in time. *I recognize that flicker!*

I turned off nearby lights, stood very still, and stared into the darkness. I called to my wife, "Dana, come here and look."

Another flicker and another. As my eyes adjusted, I felt ten years old again. How many childhood nights had I captured fireflies, put them in a jar, and drifted to sleep to their faint flickers in my room? That night came alive, decades later, as my wife and I delighted over God's subtle display of beauty.

But a strange thing happens. Every summer, the rush of life can make the flickers seem faint. They can go unnoticed. Unadjusted, distracted eyes miss the fireflies. To see this subtle, extravagant, miniature light show, I must intentionally stop and stare. I have to *want* to see it.

Gospel identity is similar. We've seen the flickers, but we need our eyes to adjust. We need to pause and focus. The longer we stare at God's display of perfect love, the brighter the reality of the gospel grows and the more amazed we become with who Jesus is and what He has done for us. Psalm 34:5 teaches that pausing to look on Jesus actually produces a radiant, glowing face.

How does a gospel identity work? How does it make us free and shape us into His image? How does it provide resources for navigating life's fragility? How does it change our relationships, our purpose, our whole life?

Amazing things happen when we allow a gospel identity to grow. We've seen the flickers—but stay with me and keep your eyes open. We are about to discover six ways a gospel identity moves from knowledge to experience.

The night is about to come alive!

"Let not the wise man boast in his wisdom, let not the mighty man boast in his might, let not the rich man boast in his riches, but let him who boasts boast in this, that he understands and knows me, that I am the Lord."

JEREMIAH 9:23–24

Chapter 9

RUN HOME

A Gospel Identity Redeems Failure

"Behold, what manner of love the Father
hath bestowed upon us, that we should
be called the sons of God."

1 JOHN 3:1 (KJV)

HIS ENERGY SPENT, he batted away the flies for the last time. His arm collapsed, spattering mud into his crusted eyes. So thick was the dried muck on his face, he stopped feeling the flies that now freely roamed his exposed skin. He was numb to the baking midday sun that intensified the stench of his pig-infested bed. For a traditional Israelite, this place—a feeding pen for swine—was the worst imaginable place to land. It was a living death, the crushing result of a modern-identity journey.

Delirious from hunger and sleeplessness, he lay motionless, half immersed in the mud and filth. Fattened pigs lazily slept nearby. His stomach wrenched itself in knots from the leathery carob pods he had choked down the last few days. He drifted in and out of awareness, sleep deprived, malnourished, alone. He lost the will to move. This was the end. He had nothing left—no resources, no one who cared, and no place to go. He was dead to others, and soon would be dead to the pigs. It had been a short ride to rock bottom.

A random moment of lucidity awakened him with a brief adrenaline rush. *I wonder if my father would hire me? I can never be his son, but perhaps he would give me a job, let me pay my debts, and live as his hired laborer.* The idea was unthinkable, but better than death.

First-century culture was built on traditional identity, and one did not dishonor his father without the rejection of the entire family and village. Not so long ago, this man had spit in his father's face, wished him dead, demanded his inheritance money, and ran recklessly from home. He had broken free from the traditional identity that his birth had imposed on him. With wild abandon, he had dived headfirst into his newly liberated, individualistic self. He had "let it go," and before long, it had all been gone.

In traditional identity structures, you don't just bounce back. You're dead to the father and dead to the family. It's over. There's no redemption or grace.

The flies continued to wander along his half-buried face. His eyes widened again as his idea circled back. *My father is kind. My walk back home will be humiliating . . .* His thoughts trailed to the day he left home. Dare he try to run *back* to the man he ran *from*? Could he expect an employer's welcome from his hated father? *If I live honorably, perhaps I can work my way back.*

Implausible hope energized him. With a handful of carob pods, he pulled his famished frame upright and slogged his way out of the pig trough. His pride broken, his future dim, his heart humiliated, he began his long trudge home.

This is why Jesus said, "For whoever would save his life will lose it, but whoever loses his life for my sake and the gospel's will save it" (Mark 8:35). He saves us from the tragedy of a life bouncing between traditional and modern identities.

· · ·

The heat of the older brother's anger rose in proportion to that of the blistering midday sun. Pausing to catch his breath, he brushed the sweat from his brow and heaved a contemptuous sigh. He imagined his younger brother resting in some exotic location, free from work and care. His thoughts returned to the furrowed field before him—his father's land. *Slave driver.*

The work had doubled after the younger brother left. How he resented his father for giving up one-third of the family's resources. *What a foolish, reckless decision. Stupid old man.* He kicked the dirt to spite the irony. *I'm the firstborn, breaking my back for my father while my younger brother is living in luxury, wasting my money.*

White-hot tears of anger mixed with white-hot midday sweat streaked his reddened face. The external heat made a good mask for the internal blaze. He had lived a long time behind that mask.

This is the way of traditional identity. Pull your weight and another's, if need be. Do your duty. Do what you must. It is involuntary. Bow before the demands of your father, leader of the family, elder of the village. The burden of traditional identity had fully fallen on this older brother, and he hated both his father and his brother for it. Though he was living obediently and faithfully, he was utterly disconnected from the love of his father. All rules, no relationship. His behavior was in line, but his heart was far from his father. He was faking it and becoming angrier every day.

• • •

Another sunrise, another sunset, another son-less day. As he did every day, the father took up his walking stick and ventured out to the precipice of the village where he could see the road meander downhill for miles to the west. He stood and stared for an hour or more as the sun slowly descended beyond the distant ridges. It wasn't the beauty of a sunset he hoped to see, but rather the beauty of repentance. He dreamed of resurrection and restoration. He knew the path below, and this evening, as every other, his eyes earnestly traced every turn, hoping that the trail that took his heart away would someday bring it back. What did he hope to see? Dust stirring. That familiar gait. A lone traveler.

For months he privately nursed his broken heart. He had lost a son, and the grief compounded daily. Though tradition would call his younger son dead, this father never stopped hoping and loving. His arms remained open. Every day he anticipated a return. Reluctantly, and against his family's urging, he gave up the inheritance and absorbed his youngest son's scorn. *If I let him go, perhaps he will understand my heart. Perhaps he will remember my love and someday return.*

Was that motion on the road below, or just the way the light played against the rocks? The father squinted into the distance. Dust rose from the path in measured rhythms. *Someone is walking toward the village.* His heart climbed into his throat. Did he dare to hope?

As the distant figure slowly came into focus, tears began to blur the old man's view. This was no stranger. He recognized that stride, and he could no longer constrain the love bound up within. In a radical break from traditional culture, he gathered up his fatherly robe, dropped his walking stick, and broke into a full-on sprint. Losing all sense of dignity or austerity, he recklessly barreled down the descending path—fighting for secure footing in the dusty rock flow, but alive with redemptive passion. He rushed toward his son, arms flailing, calling his name, heart aflame. Ignoring the swine filth, the stench, and the sweat, he threw his arms around his boy and began to kiss his neck, washing him in tears of compassion.

Imagine a love that is willing to kiss filth. Imagine the humiliation of a father absorbing his son's sin and walking his fallen heart back home again. Imagine the condemnation he would face for welcoming the outcast and for showering him in flagrant, fatherly love—the ring, the robe, the fatted calf, a welcome-home party.

The penitent son never finished his well-rehearsed script: "Father, I'm not worthy to be called your son . . ." Repentance brought immediate restoration. Though undeserved, sonship was lavishly conferred. Inheritance—one-third of the *remaining* family estate—was restored. Extravagant, unconditional love was poured out in abundance and grace. The son's identity *as son* was firmly reestablished by the father's authority.

Since his birth, this son had been well loved. All of his life he had *received* that love. Even in his "death" he was loved. But in this swine-defiled embrace, being called "son" went to a new depth. It became something more wonderful and beautiful. Being brought back into the heart of the father was beyond his expectation or imagination. The words revived his long-emaciated heart: "*This my son*" (Luke 15:24).

For the first time ever, the younger brother actually *experienced and understood* his father's love—and it melted his heart. We would say it *redefined* him.

• • •

Dusk brought a welcomed end to another long workday. As the exhausted older brother approached the house, he was puzzled by the sounds of music and dancing. He called ahead to a servant, "What's all the celebration?"

"Your brother has returned home, and your father has restored him and declared this night to be a celebration of his safe return!"

His heart seethed. Gritting his teeth, he stopped cold, blood boiling. *After all of my hard work and honor, after all of that kid's disrespect and dishonor, after giving away one-third of our resources to this traitor—how dare he! I deserve that inheritance. I deserve the celebration. I am the good son. That deserter has no place in this family.*

"Are you coming in?" the well-meaning servant asked.

Mask off, the burning inside overflowed. Enraged, the older brother stormed away.

Seconds later, in untraditional humility and love, the father left the party and approached the steaming older brother, pleading with him to join the party. But the son's heart was unrelenting with years of growing resentment.

"All these years I have served you!" the older brother screamed at his father. "Never one time have I broken your rules or failed your demands! And never one time have you given me a party with my friends! But as soon as this betrayer returns home, after wasting our money, you welcome him with extravagance!"

The father was incredulous, as were Jesus' hearers as He related this story. "My son, *everything* I have is already yours. You are always with me. Come inside and celebrate the restoration of your brother."

The older son was equally disconnected from his father's love, choosing to stew in anger rather than rest in unconditional love.

This is not the story of a good son and a bad one, or that of a faithful son and an unfaithful one. This is the story of two angry sons, both alienated from true love, both demonizing their father, and both defying him. One rebels within a traditional identity. The other rebels in a modern identity. This is a story of a loving father absorbing his sons' failures and inviting them into his heart of radical love.

Which brother are you most like?

• • •

You can find the story in Luke 15:11–32. Both sons resented their father. Neither of them had recently *experienced* his love, though they were the *recipients* of it. Neither of them truly *understood* his heart. One worked to control material blessings by hard work; the other worked to break free from perceived bondage.

The older brother related to his father through obedience motivated by gaining possession of his father's wealth. The younger brother related to his father through bondage motivated by breaking free into individual freedom. The older brother was stuck in a traditional identity and viewed his father merely as one to be exploited, leveraged for gain. The younger was steeped in a modern identity and viewed his father as one to be excoriated and escaped.

Both brothers viewed the father as something other than who he truly was. Both rebelled—one quietly, internally, and the other flagrantly, externally. One rebelled in spirit. The other rebelled in action. One was self-justifying. The other was self-liberating. The older brother shouldered his traditional self and quietly grew angry and proud. He esteemed himself better than others, and internally competed for his father's favor, not realizing it was his already. The younger brother shouldered his modern self, exploited his father's goodness, and ruthlessly ran for freedom. He liberated himself and fell tragically into individualistic self-destruction.

Both *selves* are horizontal, weak, and broken. Both selves have radically misunderstood their father's love and have never rightly related to it. Both selves need to repent and run home to their father's heart.

Much of my life I was taught to be like the older brother, not the younger. Unfortunately, that's sort of what happened.

WHAT DOES JESUS' STORY TEACH US ABOUT GOSPEL IDENTITY?

Maybe you identify with the older brother—self-righteous and self-justifying. But it's been a long time since you've actually experienced your father's love. Maybe you identify with the younger brother—running defiantly into your self-realized individuality.

Jesus' story teaches us that we tend to view our relationship with Him through a traditional or modern lens. We tend to impose our view of God on Him. As a result, our vision of Him and ourselves becomes skewed and selfish. Losing sight of the gospel, we see ourselves trapped or overworked, and God as demanding and greedy. Forgetting that Jesus fulfilled the Father's demands, we will resent God for what we have made Him—a tightfisted deity withholding His best until we behave at our best.

Or we may alternately be tempted to obey Him for selfish reasons—to leverage Him for blessing. We will see God as a means to our own ends and His commands as a means of obtaining His favor for personal purposes. We will eventually tire of trying harder to do what Jesus has already done for us.

Forgetting who we are in the gospel, our identity becomes rooted in what we do for God or others rather than in what He has done for us. Our motivations change. We serve Him to secure His blessings rather than to express love and enjoy the fact that He's already given them to us. We live *for* His best rather than *from* it. When life becomes hard, we will wonder what happened. We will wonder why our Father let us down—disappointed that He didn't serve us well.

When we obey, we will compare ourselves to our younger brothers and become proud that we have not disappointed our Father as they have. We will view ourselves as worthy of His blessings and our younger brothers as deserving of His punishment. We will scorn them rather than love them. If God fails our expectations of blessings, we will secretly scorn Him as well—as though He owes us and hasn't paid up.

When we become like the younger brother, we run from the love we're actually looking for, or we view the liberty we have in Christ as something to exploit for self-gratification. We view our Father as someone to be liberated from rather than someone to run to, or we view His grace as a license to licentiousness. Either view forgets the gospel's great fulfillment of our hearts and tempts us to deify our desires over our Father. Like the younger brother, we lose sight of the lavish life we have in the Father's estate and feel that our heart could be better fulfilled far from Him. We will distrust His heart because we haven't *experienced* it.

Jesus' story teaches us that we can receive His love without truly experiencing or being transformed by it. It's not enough to know about it. It must be *experienced*. Too often I have been the older brother. Obedient. Hardworking. Viewing God through a traditional identity lens, I worked hard to live up to who I was supposed to be. Though I was aware of His grace, I was *practically* relating to God on the basis of my works for Him rather than His for me.

I've believed in Jesus for much longer than I've understood the implications of gospel identity. For a long time, it was like faint flickers in the background of my busyness. I tried to *become* for Jesus. Without realizing it, I took a *vertical* gospel and flattened it into a *horizontal* identity. I was fervent to produce for God and win the approval of God and others. But I was not growing in personal, emotional, and spiritual maturity. His love had saved me from sin but had not yet redefined my heart.

Like Peter, though I knew the gospel, it had not reshaped me. I was trying to shape myself to it rather than allowing Jesus to do the shaping. Like Peter, I was following Jesus in my own definitions, but I was still insecure in many ways. Judging by my works, you would have assumed spiritual maturity. But my heart was embarrassingly weak in the actual fruit of the Spirit (Gal. 5:22–23). My struggle to produce fruit actually prevented the healthy conditions in which fruit would grow organically.

Though I had received His love, I can't say that I had deeply experienced it.

He was patient. He accepted my flawed motives, forgave my presumptuous spirit, and even blessed the good things I was doing for Him. Like most growing followers of Jesus, my motives were mixed—some pure, some selfish, some theologically skewed.

To use the firefly metaphor, I had filled my world with the light I had created. Then He graciously turned the lights off. He broke down all of the subtle places where I had anchored my heart. When my constructed identity went dark, my unadjusted eyes began to see flickers, faint at first but growing in brightness. The profound beauty and power of a gospel identity was there all the time, but I had drowned it out with subconscious traditional and modern narratives beautifully lit with surface spirituality. I had adopted horizontal narratives and called them "Christian."

My performance for Jesus blinded me to the magnitude of His victorious battle for me. As my eyes adjusted, my sense of self grew smaller; and realizing how deeply flawed my soul is, my sense of sin and weakness grew larger. In turn, Jesus' love and work on the cross also grew larger. His work became everything and my offerings but a minuscule response.[1]

Without warning, my heart was melted by His infinite love.

Jesus' story teaches us that failure and struggle can make our Father's love experiential if we run home in repentance. The gospel isn't merely a resource to avoid hitting the bottom in life—it's our only hope when we do. From the rock bottom of failure, struggles, or loss, the gospel calls us home to His heart. Without the gospel, we would be destitute. If you are the younger brother, gospel identity says, "Repent of your rebellion and self-discovery and run home to your Father's heart."

If you are the older brother, gospel identity says, "Repent of your self-righteousness and misappropriation of your Father's love. Resolve your anger in His grace."

The story calls both sons back into the father's arms by humble repentance. Only one actually accepted the offer. In the gospel, there is never a time when you will not be welcomed back into His love. The father never stopped loving the younger son, though for a season the son refused to experience it. Likewise, our Father's love never stops. We can remove ourselves from the experience of it, but we can never lose it.

The gospel will not allow you to remain in self-loathing over failure because Jesus absorbed your failures and granted you His success. But neither will it allow you to puff up in pride because your salvation and personal value were accomplished by Jesus, not by you. Experiencing the gospel humbles you organically because you know, apart from Jesus, you are hopeless. But that humility is not false or self-deprecating because you know Jesus considered you worth dying for.

• • •

How are you running? If defined by success, you run from failure. If defined by hurt, you run from pain. If defined by age, you run from time. If defined by ethnicity, you run from racial differences. If defined by ability, you run from mistakes. If defined by money, you run from financial loss. This list goes on.

Whatever *defines* you forces you to run from whatever *threatens* you. A gospel identity invites you to stop running *from* and start running *to*. Run into His love—His acceptance, security, and significance. He reorders your heart. A right relationship with your Father will flow into a right relationship with yourself and others. When His love melts your heart, everything else grows clearer.

Paul understood running home: "Brothers, I do not consider that I have made it my own. But one thing I do: forgetting what lies behind and straining forward to what lies ahead, I press on toward the goal for the prize of the upward call of God in Christ Jesus" (Phil. 3:13–14).

How does God drive the gospel from my head to my heart?

Let's move from "finding to flourishing." Now that we have begun to see the wonders of a gospel identity, you're probably thinking: *I long to be this new person!*

We can't get there on our own. We can't force it or will it into reality. We don't need to despair the fact that it's a struggle or a growing process. It's really not up to us, but we can participate in His process. Jesus called it "following Him" (Luke 9:23).

Half of this book was written on a study trip to the Holy Land. It's been surreal to write about the Sea of Galilee while sitting on its shoreline. Writing these particular words, I happen to be sitting in a café in Old City Jerusalem after a confusing morning of navigating a maze of narrow stone streets. With a backpack and a simple map, I dodged tourists, traversed markets, and made myself dizzy with wrong turns. Several times I ended up at the same gate where I entered the city. At one point I found myself at a dead end near Temple Mount, staffed with well-armed guards. Doing the Old City alone is complicated.

But I'm here with my friend Kurt who knows the city well. When I'm with Kurt, I just tag along. I don't worry about where I am or what turn to take. I don't stress over maps and directions. I relax and enjoy the journey. I have a simple strategy actually: *Keep Kurt in view! Stay close to Kurt! Oh, no, where's Kurt?*

My reference point is Kurt. As long as he is in view, my travels in the Holy Land feel secure, well planned, and fun. A gospel identity makes Jesus your reference point in life—not yourself or others. With Him in view, your journey will be secure and delightful. You can stop clinging to others and actually start loving, enjoying, and blessing them.

Periodically, Kurt looks at me with a knowing look and says, "C'mon, follow me." When he does, I spring into motion, knowing the journey will lead someplace awesome. Yesterday, we climbed a hill, passed through a barbed-wire fence, and stood on Ahab's palace wall in Jezreel. When Kurt says, "Follow me," I trust him and stay close, always glad I did.

That's how your life's journey with Jesus should be—it's a secure adventure. Life leaves you alone with a backpack full of rocks and no map. Religion merely adds more rocks to the pack.

But in the gospel, Jesus steps ahead of you, shoulders your pack, turns to you with a warm smile, and says, "C'mon, follow Me!" Stay close, keep Jesus in view, and enjoy the adventure.

A bunch of angry seagulls made me see this more clearly. C'mon, follow me, and I'll tell you about it.

"Follow me, and I will make you . . ."

**JESUS TO PETER AND ANDREW
IN MATTHEW 4:19**

Part Three

FLOURISHING

*"The righteous flourish like the palm tree
and grow like a cedar in Lebanon.
They are planted in the house of the LORD;
they flourish in the courts of our God."*
PSALM 92:12–13

GOSPEL IDENTITY—We know about it, but how do we *experience* it?

This is who we want to be. How can we flourish in it? How is this made real?

It happens when we actually *experience* our Father's strong arms around us and His warm kisses on our necks. Our new identity flourishes as we know Him the way His first followers did, and as we entrust ourselves to His patient, lifetime cultivation.

God broadly uses two things over a lifetime to shape us into His image—*providential experiences* and *personal cultivation*. The experiences are involuntary; our responses are voluntary. The good news is, He does the work as we allow Him to.

It's time to begin flourishing like Jesus' first followers.

Chapter 10

FACE UPWARD

A Gospel Identity Reshapes Hardship

"I had been my whole life a bell, and never knew it
until at that moment I was lifted and struck."[1]

ANNIE DILLARD

I'M SITTING IN A BEACH CHAIR contemplating life, identity, and the
difference between the strength of gospel identity and the weakness
of other options. After an intense season of ministry, this break has
been restorative.

I'm nibbling on pretzel sticks, minding my own business. The
emerald gulf lazily laps its warm water over sugar-white sands—
each gentle fold tossing fresh sand and small crabs into the foamy
surf. My snack bag crackles in the morning breeze. The salty air clears
my thoughts. The salty snack pleases my taste buds. The crackling is
a clarion call in the world of feathered fowls—*Ahoy, snacks ashore!*

The first to arrive are a couple of unintelligent pigeons to dote
around my chair, heads bobbing, eyes bugged out. Then a single

seagull arrives. He lands five yards in front of me, stares me down, and squawks his demand. I imagine him screaming, "Pretzels, NOW!" I stare back, intrigued by the standoff.

A second gull lands, then a third. The first turns and hisses at the other two who had apparently stepped into his personal space. I think the hiss meant, "Two feet, pals. Keep the zone wide."

They know the sound of crackling snack bags in these parts. They smell carbs in the wind. On a seagull's luckiest days, tourists take walks and leave snack bags unattended. That cellophane bag gives way in two pecks, and it's a hometown buffet. Now, their eyes suggest *Take a walk, pal; you know you want a walk. We'll watch the pretzels.*

Tauntingly, I gently draw a single small pretzel stick from the bag and flick it to my right. Pandemonium. Squawk fest. Wings flutter madly. Everybody pounces, but only one gets the pretzel. The winner prances away while the losers return to the zone— now shifted five yards to the right.

Immediately, twenty more gulls find their places in the formation—each strategically standing equidistant from others, giving everybody a fair shot. They look like a ball team assuming positions on the field.

Random squawking and hissing explodes if the two-foot space is breached. Every gull is poised. They are the symphony. I am the conductor. My baton, a tiny pretzel. The pigeons are wandering aimlessly, missing the whole orchestration.

Silence—except for the surf and slight breeze. Every gull is motionless.

So I wait. And wait.

One gull breaks from the group. He's standing over my shoulder, to the left, at least ten yards from any other. I muse over what he's thinking—*I'm going to beat the system. Calculating this guy's throw, the wind direction, and pretzel loft, my math says pretzels are coming to the back left.* I'm guessing he's got a scientific calculator and aced advanced math.

To spite him—the calculus genius—I throw the next stick to the back right where no gull is standing. Half the group laughs at the scientist. The others dive-bomb the pretzel. Again, one wins and struts away as all others reset formation.

How obsessively they stand poised—all for a long shot at a short pretzel. Directly behind them, the surf is delivering up fresh sand crabs by the dozens—the equivalent of a crab-leg buffet.

There is irony in this madness—both theirs and ours. Their Creator has provided a shoreline of delightful soft-shelled treats and sushi snacks. I, the imposter, have taunted them with bits of nothing. To their backs, a buffet. In front of them, just my torturous tomfoolery.

I mess with their minds. They fall for it.

It draws them into squawking, hissing, threatening postures as they compete. It's a gull-eat-gull world in my small symphony, where carbs distract from crabs.

My pretzels—indeed my malice—transform them. They forget who and what they are. They fight for dominance. They ravage one another for pretzels. Then, one by one, they lose interest in my diversion and return to restfully being gulls. They move from high-strung to happy—content in the surf for which they were created. They find abundance. Every gull finds its own provision in its own place—peaceably being exactly what its Creator designed. Hissing ceases. Happiness returns.

When facing the provision where water meets sand, they find fullness. When facing a stranger, they descend into scarcity and struggle. Their *orientation* determines their *experience*. They are designed to soar over a million sandy miles of fresh feasts, but one crackling snack bag draws them into turmoil over bits of nothing. It's a struggle between who they really are and who I distract them to be.

Now, let's get a bird's-eye view of ourselves.

Like a distracted seagull, I am harassed and drawn from my God-given identity into my fragile self. Carbs or crabs. Hissing, posturing, pettiness, and worry versus loving, resting fullness, and joy. One is hopelessly enslaved to drama and emotion, the other wonderfully free and grounded in truth.

When basking in Jesus' gospel provision, I am free to soar and feast in His abundant love. Distracted by false identity narratives, I am drawn back into a pretzel fight. Every day presents the same choice, and every day offers the same freedom. But breaking free is not instinctive at first. It's a patient, growing journey—costly, but worth it. It's a daily decision to face upward, outward, and forward as the psalmist wrote, "My voice shalt thou hear in the morning, O LORD; in the morning will I direct my prayer unto thee, and will look up" (Ps. 5:3 KJV).

• • •

Like those seagulls, Peter and John hissed at each other. Their fragile selves were highly competitive and comparative. Their eyes were always aimed horizontally at each other in tense ways. John, nicknamed "son of thunder," repeatedly rehearsed Peter's failures. Peter continually compared himself to John. When Jesus prophesied Peter's martyrdom (John 21:18–22), his odd response was to point to John and say, "Well, what about this guy?" (Like, *If I have to die, then shouldn't he?*) They squawked over fragments of fake identity such as, *Who would be more prominent in the coming kingdom?* or *Who has to die first?*

But Jesus has a way of clearing and lifting—reorienting—our vision. In Mark 8:25, He did to a blind man what He desires to do for us: "Then Jesus . . . opened his eyes, his sight was restored, and he saw everything clearly." How I long to see everything clearly in the light of who Jesus is and who He says I am. More so, how I long to face upward in my new identity rather than being drawn into frivolous pretzel fights. That drama is merely a mind game. When I leave it, I never miss it.

FORTY DAYS OF TRANSFORMATION

For forty days, Jesus stayed after His resurrection—forty redefining days. Metaphors fail. This wasn't a light bulb coming on in the heads of Jesus' followers—it was a billion light bulbs. This was an epic awakening, not merely mind-blowing, but nuclear—a radical transformation of the psyches of Jesus' friends.

I'm curious about these days. Someday in heaven, if there's a big video screen, I want to grab a month's worth of buttered popcorn, recline in heaven's softest recliner, and binge-watch these forty days.

Jesus did life with His friends for nearly seven weeks, speaking to them of the things "about the kingdom of God" (Acts 1:3). This time they really listened! Their filter wasn't a geopolitical kingdom, but something like, *This is God. He died for me; He rose again; and He's telling me who I am, what I am created to do, and where I am going when it's all over.*

On the fortieth day, as they walked to the Mount of Olives near Bethany, Jesus told them not to worry about the times or seasons but to focus on giving the gospel to the world. Then, He disappeared. His followers gawked—eyes wide, jaws dropped—as He ascended into the clouds, leaving them with final instructions to wait for His Spirit to help them.

The return walk to Jerusalem was marked with extraordinary joy. Ironic. Just forty-two days prior, these followers were numb with depression, biting their nails to the nubs, hiding in fear. Now they were dancing in the streets and slapping high fives. Their Lord was gone. Their dreams dashed. Their plans were completely overwritten. Two empires wanted them eradicated, and their response was to gush forth in laughter—impervious to their enemies, immune to worry, and impenetrable to fear.

If you asked them how or why the transformation took place, they would probably look at you incredulously—*Are you kidding? He defied death and flew away. He's coming back, and He's given us kingdom assignments until then. We win, and we're here on purpose until He returns. Nothing can touch this!*

Peter later wrote that they had been born into a "living hope" and that we are given precious promises as partakers of a new, divine nature (1 Peter 1:3; 2 Peter 1:4). Truly their psyches had become new, and it changed their relationships. Everybody else looks very different through the lens of your own gospel identity. For the first time, you see them as Jesus sees them.

This time they waited happily and peaceably. Every day, the same space that had been silent with despair a month and a half earlier was now alive with laughter and celebratory worship. Every day they walked to the temple celebrating their new reality, delirious with hope and fortified with new strength that had dawned upon them.

Please get this. *It dawned; it was not "dutied" into existence. And now their love for each other overshadowed their competition with each other. Hurtful gulls became happy gulls.*

It beautifully materialized by God's Spirit—uncontrived. It was not coerced by religious dictates. It was organically realized by God, to everyone's surprise and delight. Jesus' followers willingly allowed the transformation to take place by faith, even as we are instructed, "And let the peace of Christ rule in your hearts" (Col. 3:15).

Will we be drawn into pretzel-stick identities, fighting for our two-foot zones of security and significance? Will we go on competing and comparing with others over pointless trivialities? Or will we let the air currents of gospel identity lift us and turn us upward, outward, and forward toward God's shoreline of abundance?

• • •

The stench was unbearable. The darkness impenetrable. The threat tangible. Peter and John sat together in their dungeon-esque accommodations—compliments of the Jewish cartel that executed Jesus. A random rat scurried by, and muffled voices of guards were faintly heard down sandstone halls. Distant torch lights cast a disparate hint of color into their vile prison space.

A few weeks had passed since Jesus ascended. Was this prison cell the end for Peter and John? If so, what a short but glorious run it had been. The followers of Jesus had fully broken free from their old selves and had begun to live out of their new gospel definitions. Fear and cowardice had been transformed into courage and joy. Jesus' reality had made them free to be who He created and called them to be.

Rather than hiss at each other, Peter and John willingly served together. Rather than compete, they collaborated. Jesus and His Spirit comprehensively recalibrated their identities; and those new selves were activated, thrust upon an unsuspecting Jerusalem. The church at Jerusalem exploded into a forceful new reality at Pentecost, the Jewish feast of thanks.

Flawed Peter stood and realized his new self as a "fisher of men." The first "casting of the net" drew three thousand new believers, and the second celebrated five thousand just days later. The city quickly became home to thousands of new Christians, sweeping the population into a heated controversy over Jesus and His newly audacious followers. After the feast, many others returned home to faraway regions, starting Christian communities in many other cities.

Some days later, when Peter was going to the temple to pray and preach, John stepped up and said, "I'll go with you." Hissing turned to helping. Imagine the others marveling at their relational transformation. Gone was the competition and comparison. These men were operating from new identities and blessing others together.

In Acts 3, 4, and 5, they healed a blind man *together*. They preached the gospel in the temple *together*. They were arrested *together*. When cross-examined, rather than deny or shift blame on one another, they displayed the gospel (4:13). When threatened, rather than shrink into intimidation and silence, they courageously declared, "For we cannot but speak of what we have seen and heard" (4:20). When beaten and released, rather than hide in terror, they loudly worshiped Jesus. Rather than mope, they celebrated.

I would have prayed, "Lord, deliver me from these enemies." Old Peter would have prayed, "Lord, give them John first!" But together they prayed something like, "Lord, give us more courage to speak the gospel" (see 4:23–29). New selves honored Jesus and blessed others with new unity and audacious faith. They actually enjoyed it!

It all led to that dark night in prison and the genuine possibility of a mock trial and bloody execution the following day. But this would be a night they would never forget. In the darkness of the prison cell, they felt the presence of a third person. Then a whisper broke the silence, "Follow me." *Have we drifted off to sleep? Is this a dream? Are we hallucinating?*

Motion, the clanking of metal. This third person abruptly unlatched the lock, swung the cell door open, and moved swiftly down the corridor toward the exit. Guards seemed oblivious. No alarm. No shouts. No restraints. Peter, John, and their strange new companion walked out brazenly into the barren midnight streets of old Jerusalem. Fresh summer air expanded their lungs. Joy. Freedom.

This is no dream. It's real!

Then the stranger revealed his identity, "I am God's angel, sent to release you. Go back to the temple and continue telling the people all of the words of this new life" (see 5:17–42).

As fast as he appeared, he was gone. Peter and John instinctively embraced, overwhelmed with the new reality. Impenetrable. Indestructible. Having lost themselves, they had found new selves, freely looking upward. They had begun to soar into being who they were created and commissioned to be. Free to flourish. Free from fear.

LAVISH NEW LIFE AND LOVE

This is the lavish new life that Jesus' first followers experienced. At every hard place, their new selves grew stronger, deeper, and more confident. They were characterized by indestructible joy—focused, purposeful, and buoyant. They irreversibly discovered who they really were. They gladly and generously loved each other.

A gospel identity gave them—*and gives us*—a remarkable new quality of life in spite of harsh circumstances. They experienced *undying drive and direction*, rock-solid new purpose that remained unshaken in the face of grave threats. They discovered *uncommon confidence and resilience*, empowered by God's Spirit and emboldened by the reality of the resurrection. They operated with *unbreakable joy and optimism*, abounding in spite of intimidation tactics, abuse, slander, and the threat of death.

They fully embraced Jesus' teaching that "all they can really do is kill your body; but in the end, not one hair of your head will be hurt" (see Luke 21:16–19). Like never before, by God's Spirit, they took possession of their souls, knowing their souls could never be lost (Luke 21:19).

They were no longer living *for* a fragile identity; they were living *from* a strong one. And God used hardship to reveal their new strength. This is the power of facing upward and outward in gospel identity. Our view of things changes, which means our psyches change. Our perspective changes, and we see all of life differently.

The same storms that destroy a balsa wood life serve to make real life—even with its prisons—more adventurous and meaningful. Like hard drives reformatted, fragile identities are overwritten by gospel grace and all its implications. Our orientation shifts from horizontal to vertical, inward to outward. We stop hissing and stressing over small bites of life. We face the wide shoreline of God's grace and feast on His fullness. We rest in being our truest, redeemed selves; we are safe in our Savior, flourishing in His good love, and peaceable toward others—even those who hurt us.

The taunting stranger in the beach chair is rendered powerless and irrelevant. We walk away from the mind game and enter the provision of our Redeemer. Nothing can separate us from His love (Rom. 8:35–39). Our identity in Him is sealed permanently and irrevocably (Eph. 1:13; Gal. 4:5).

This reality is experientially forceful, as we saw in Peter and John. It infuses our hearts with new strength and rearranges our psyches in the same way a seagull facing the seashore behaves differently than one facing my beach chair. Like a Category 5 hurricane rearranges a landscape, the gospel rearranges your heart, but in good ways, transforming the way you do life and relationships. In the gospel, the psyche moves from horizontal weakness to vertical strength.

We live *from* flourishing, not *for* it.

We give *from* fullness, rather than seek it.

We serve *from* God's favor rather than *for* it.

A gospel identity doesn't merely demand that we make ourselves new and then live up to it. It *declares* us new and empowers us to live from newness in authentic ways. Jesus gives us a new psyche that doesn't try to *be* new; it simply is. It's not a new burden to work at; it's a new reality that shows up. It can be cultivated but not coerced.

It simply takes looking upward and outward. Change your orientation and put on gospel lenses. In every circumstance, ask God, "How does the gospel enable me to view and respond to this situation?" Hebrews teaches us to "[look] to Jesus, the founder and perfecter of our faith" and to "consider him who endured from sinners such hostility against himself, so that [we] may not grow weary or fainthearted" (12:2–3).

Until we stop fighting for pretzel sticks and walk away from the taunter, we will never discover the seashore. We were created for a buffet, not crumbs; resting, not squawking; feasting, not competing. So let's face a new direction and cultivate this new identity.

God uses failure and struggle to invite us to run into His arms. God uses hardship and suffering to cause us to look upward and outward.

You're going to like the next one.

"One thing have I asked of the LORD, that will I seek after: that I may dwell in the house of the LORD all the days of my life, to gaze upon the beauty of the LORD."

PSALM 27:4

Chapter 11

STAND UP

A Gospel Identity Resolves Fear

"The LORD is my light and my salvation;
whom shall I fear?"

PSALM 27:1

IT HAD BEEN A LONG WINTER, and Chad hadn't gone swimming since last summer when he was three. The pool sprawling before him must have looked like a vast and dangerous ocean to his four-year-old eyes. He stood at the water's edge, well covered in sunscreen and decked in new swim gear designed after his favorite cartoon characters. His floating vest made him unsinkable, but that didn't matter. He didn't trust it, and he didn't trust me either.

Noticing his fear, I grabbed his hand, scooped him up in my arms, and said, "Come on, buddy! Papa will take you." His fear swelled as, without his approval, I stepped into the fresh water. Instinctively, my grandson wrapped both of his arms and legs around my body. I could feel his heart rate increase and his tiny lungs expand frantically. His mind raced with the dangerous possibilities before us as we sloshed our way toward the "lazy river."

Two worlds collided in this moment—Chad's fearful risk-aversion, and Papa's confident reality. In Chad's world, lazy rivers sweep children into raging torrents of destruction. In Papa's world, lazy rivers are fabulous fun. Chad's worldview is shaping a terrified psyche. Papa is giving Chad a new psyche that can enjoy vacation.

As we waded into the current, Chad's grip strengthened. "Papa, don't let me go!"

"Chad, you're okay. I've got you." My warm, grandfatherly tones made no difference to his fear. He barely heard me. His fear was strong, and the voices in his head were loud. His eyes darted; his breaths quickened.

My heart felt his fear and desperately wanted to calm and release him from *himself*. The more I talked, the less he heard. Every second he grew more tense. This family vacation was suddenly no fun for him. No matter how cool his "floaties" looked, apparently floating is for the fish! All he wanted was solid ground.

Gently, I peeled Chad's feet away from my waist and took his arms in mine. His panic grew as he felt the gap between us. He grasped, but I resisted, softly lowering him toward the water.

"Chad, stand up," I coached, to no avail.

He frantically tried to climb back into my embrace. "No, Papa, don't let me go. Hold me!"

Ironically, we were standing in two-and-a-half feet of water, well below Chad's head, and the mild current would have been no trouble. But his mind was racing so fast, I couldn't lock his attention on the facts. His *actual* reality was overwhelmed by his *fear-constructed* view. Truth was shouted down by feelings, and

Papa needed to orchestrate some redefining event to overpower Chad's psyche.

Perhaps God has orchestrated similar events in your life for the same reason.

He's not going to like this, I thought to myself. But I knew what I needed to do. It was the only thing I *could* do to break down Chad's fear and ground him in truth. I had to let him go for a split second, and when I did, the look on his face was heartbreaking. *Papa, how could you?* His eyes widened; he cried out, sure he would be swept away.

It's important to note, never once was Chad vulnerable to actual danger or outside of my immediate care. But in that moment, he had no sense of my love. Then Papa did something unthinkable. I reached under the water, grabbed Chad's free-floating ankles, and began to pull them down. This time the terror-stricken look in his eyes seemed to scream, *Help! My papa is trying to kill me!* This emotion was but a fraction of a second as Chad's four-year-old feet quickly landed on the solid ground six inches below. His frantic kicking for survival halted. With my face mere inches from his, I smiled into his eyes. He paused. His confusion cleared.

"Stand up," I whispered, trying to stare tender confidence into him. His fear fled, and his face softened. He half-smiled and briefly looked side to side, a bit embarrassed. Then he looked back at me, released his death grip, and slowly stood with broadening confidence. I'll never forget what he said next.

"Ohhh . . ." became a wide smile.

That moment transformed Chad's entire vacation. He moved from fearing to fun, and spent the next week playing, sliding, floating, and standing on the solid ground just under the water. His new confidence transformed his psyche as the gospel transforms ours.

As Papa used Chad's anxiety and fear to lead him into strength and joy, would you imagine God can do the same with your anxieties and fears?

LEARNING TO STAND UP

This is why Paul, from his prison in Rome, challenged the suffering believers in Philippi to experience "being confident of this very thing, that he which hath begun a good work in you will perform it until the day of Jesus Christ" (Phil. 1:6 KJV). Confidence is the solid ground of the gospel, and joy is the unrestrainable result of standing in it. God used the suffering of first-century believers to ground them experientially in gospel identity. Their world was unpredictable, and gospel hope held their psyches together. Paul taught believers in his letter to the Philippians that they could "rejoice in the Lord always" (Phil. 4:4), regardless of their swirling life circumstances.

Here's the catch. The suffering, the struggle, was the *catalyst*. It is what made Jesus' followers *cognizant* of their new durability. If God hadn't given them a sense of instability at the surface, they would not have experienced His stability beneath it. This is why David could write, "Many are the afflictions of the righteous, but the LORD delivers him out of them all" (Ps. 34:19). And Paul came to understand, "For this light momentary affliction is preparing for us an eternal weight of glory beyond all comparison" (2 Cor. 4:17).

Consider all that changed in Chad. He didn't work at change. He couldn't force his emotions into order. He needed a new set of definitions to organically reorder his psyche. A class on physics wouldn't have helped. A book on water safety or a lecture on overcoming fear would have been useless in the moment.

Jesus' first followers were similarly redefined. Jesus had instructed them often, but gospel hope sprung to reality in anxious times. He applied the gospel to their struggles, and it reordered their identities. In profound distress, Paul confidently stood and declared, "But I do not account my life of any value nor as precious to myself, if only I may finish my course and the ministry that I received from the Lord Jesus, to testify to the gospel of the grace of God" (Acts 20:24). The power of the gospel awakens new identity—an "Ohhh" moment—as we learn to stand on the solid ground below our swirling world.

Jesus calls us to delight our way through life—impervious to fear and anxiety. But we are so busy kicking our feet and screaming for help that we rarely let our feet touch bottom. We've never discovered that we can actually *stand*. Sometimes, in grace, He forcibly grabs our ankles and plants our feet in His truth. But there's another way. We can voluntarily stand in the gospel. In every anxiety we can apply the gospel to our surface situation—to filter and process our experience by what we *know* is true, rather than by what we *fear* or *feel*. This is to allow the peace of God to rule our hearts (Col. 3:15), and it's why Jesus said to His disciples, "Peace I leave with you; my peace I give to you" (John 14:27).

Learning to stand in the gospel is a liberating process. It allows us to fully realize our uniqueness or God-given dreams and also willingly embrace our responsibilities to others "as unto the Lord" (Eph. 5:22; 6:5; Col. 3:23). A gospel identity fulfills the longings of our hearts without the accompanying fragility of other identities. It's all upside and no downside. New security, acceptance, and significance—in abundance—frees us from our fragile selves. This is why Jesus taught His disciples: "If you abide in my word, you are truly my disciples, and you will know the truth, and the truth will set you free. . . . So if the Son sets you free, you will be free indeed" (John 8:31–32, 36).

Standing in a gospel identity is not a onetime event, but a daily decision. Our world may overwhelm us, but solid ground is always just beneath us. The gospel undergirds us with new and permanent confidence that "the LORD is on my side; I will not fear. What can man do to me?" (Ps. 118:6).

NEW SOLID GROUND IN JERUSALEM

After Jesus' resurrection, His followers began to operate *from* strength and affirmation rather than *for* it. They ceased being defined by first-century structures. Their definitions were no longer anchored to religious success or failure, political victory or defeat, physical life or death. Their identities were anchored solely to Jesus and His radical new reality. He became so real that they were organically and systemically transformed.

Can you imagine the chapter titles of an autobiography on Peter's life prior to the resurrection?

I'm a Galilean.
I'm a fisherman.
I'm a friend of Jesus.
I'm an associate of a King.
I'm in the top three.
I'm a key leader.
I'm a competitor.

I'm a warrior.
I'm a failure.
I'm a coward.
I'm an outcast.
I'm broken.
I guess I'm just a Galilean and a fisherman again.
Honestly, I'm not really sure who I am.

When Peter's life-canvas was finally blank, he understood who Jesus was, and it comprehensively redefined him. He moved from being a weak man *pretending* to be strong to being a humble follower of Jesus operating in His very real strength. At last, Jesus could activate the true script for Peter's life.

Paul described it beautifully in Galatians 2:20: "I have been crucified with Christ. It is no longer I who live, but Christ who lives in me. And the life I now live in the flesh I live by faith in the Son of God, who loved me and gave himself for me." Do you see the losing, finding, and flourishing?

"I have been crucified with Christ"—there's the loss of self.

"It is no longer I who live, but Christ who lives in me"—there's the finding of a new self in Jesus.

"The Son of God"—rooted in who Jesus is.

"Who loved me and gave himself for me"—and what He has done.

Because of the gospel, a multitude of people in Jerusalem experienced an "Ohhh" moment similar to Chad's. First-century life in the Greco-Roman world was dog-eat-dog. Wealthy and well-connected people fought for dominance, hoarded resources, and spurned the poor or outcast. In Jerusalem, powerful people oppressed and enslaved poor people. Survival was daily, difficult work.

Imagine the relational complexity of new believers from every ethnic and socioeconomic strata of Jerusalem suddenly thrust together in the same worship spaces. The strong and the weak, Jewish and Gentile, rich and poor, successful and failed, bond and free, educated and ignorant brought together as equals in Jesus. Hierarchies were flattened in the gospel as religion gave way to new gospel relationships. It was a radical reordering of society, a cultural phenomenon.

Luke describes this new society in Acts 4:

> Now the full number of those who believed were of one heart and soul [*psuche*], and no one said that any of the things that belonged to him was his own, but they had everything in common. And with great power the apostles were giving their testimony to the resurrection of the Lord Jesus, and great grace was upon them all. There was not a needy person among them, for as many as were owners of lands or houses sold them and brought the proceeds of what was sold and laid it at the apostles' feet, and it was distributed to each as any had need. Thus Joseph, who was also called by the apostles Barnabas (which means son of encouragement), a Levite, a native of Cyprus, sold a field that belonged to him and brought the money and laid it at the apostles' feet. (vv. 32–37)

Luke is not necessarily giving us directives for twenty-first-century life. He's describing the new soul (psyche) that material-ized from the gospel. Selfish people became selfless. Disagreeable people became "of one heart." Greedy people stopped hoarding resources and began to share with those in need. Fearful people began to speak courageously of Jesus. Grace abounded from previously graceless hearts.

One of the greatest evidences of these new gospel identities was the reordering of material values. In a society where resources were precious, self-centered people became abundance-minded. Hoarders saw their material possessions through a gospel lens. Being given "more than enough" in Jesus, promised all the resources of heaven, and adopted by an infinite Father, they began to see their immediate supply as expendable and useful. Generous new desires grew from formerly greedy hearts. Their security went vertical, making their possessions expendable. New believers stopped scrambling in the swirling currents of physical neediness and decided rather to stand in God's provision. Sincere believers voluntarily liquidated their excess possessions—houses, lands, things they didn't need—for the sake of gospel mission.

This was an astounding development in a culture so typically averse to it.

Among the great irony was a Grecian Jew and religious leader named Barnabas—nicknamed "Encourager." It was unlikely that Barnabas would leave the traditional religious structure to follow a self-proclaimed Messiah who died. It was even more unlikely that a religious leader would sacrifice his material wealth. In this traditional culture, wealth was viewed as God's reward to those most deserving.

Imagine the wonder that filtered through the city when Barnabas sold his own land and brought the money to Jesus' disciples for gospel ministry. His heart was pure. His new psyche was generous. His new vertical value system reordered horizontal priorities. Barnabas wasn't seeking attention, and nobody preached a series on "Seven Principles of Financial Blessing." He simply stood up and found solid ground under his feet that happened to be more solid than his saving accounts and investment portfolio.

The first word of the next chapter of Acts is "But" (chapter 5).

All was not well in the young church. As a new wave of gospel generosity unfolded, selling stuff became "the thing to do." In a world of traditional identity, you "do" the "things you're supposed to do" to sustain your identity. Affirmation, acceptance, and favor are all found in living up to or exceeding expectations. Motives don't matter; it's all about duty. Purity of heart is irrelevant; appearance is everything. Fake it if you have to, as long as you fit the mold and meet or exceed expectations.

A traditional identity is stoked feverishly in a room full of people who agree on similar behaviors and then mutually affirm each other for performing those behaviors better than those outside of the room. It's a sad game that we are all tempted to play.

This is what happened with a man named Ananias and his wife, Sapphira. They brought their traditional identities into a gospel environment, attempting to exploit the new church for admiration and self-gratification. Perhaps they wanted prominence or notoriety. Perhaps they needed to "keep up with Barnabas." Rather than stand in gospel identity, they allowed the pressure of traditional culture to pull them into pretense and fakery. They sold their land voluntarily, but agreed to lie about the amount of money they gave. Though they were free to give all, part, or none of it, they chose to put on a show.

It's a shocking story because moments after they publicly lied, they were providentially "taken out." God took their lives, making a very public statement: "Don't use My church to construct a weak identity." Luke describes the shock wave that rippled through the city this way: "And great fear came upon the whole church and upon all who heard of these things. . . . None of the rest dared join them, but the people held them in high esteem. And more than ever believers were added to the Lord, multitudes of both men and women" (Acts 5:11, 13–14).

This passage describes three things that happened to the new church after this spectacle. First, believers became afraid to fake it. Pretense, duplicity, and relational insecurities gave way to absolute authenticity. Second, a contingency of wealthy, politically motivated people walked away and refused to join them. They discovered the gospel is a pesticide to fakery. Third, purity of motives gave free course for the gospel to change lives, and many new believers were born. God's Spirit was unrestrained. Believers moved out of God's way and let the gospel run free. When the gospel runs free, grace pours forth, life-change abounds, and new identities spring up. Hearts, marriages, families, and churches become healthy and flourish.

There was a massive contrast between the early followers of Jesus and the traditional, religious world of first-century Jerusalem. That same contrast remains vivid today in a gospel vs. religion comparison. Barnabas was standing on the solid ground of his new identity, genuinely and generously giving himself to gospel ministry. On the other hand, Ananias and Sapphira were stuck in the fragility of traditional identity and gripped with pride and insecurity, which drove them to lie to God and His church, abruptly shortening their lives. God prevented a steady stream of politics, envy, and judgmentalism from sweeping into His new community of growing gospel identities.

I love Barnabas. Every time we see him, he's growing and serving in the gospel. His "Ohhh" experience set him free from traditional, performance-based living and made him free to be his true self, ministering God's grace wherever God placed him. He was comfortable in his own skin, in many diverse environments, with many differing people. He blessed, encouraged, and befriended. He was uniquely flexible, durable, and relationally mature—from Jerusalem to Antioch to Tarsus back to Antioch and then into Turkey on Paul's first missionary journey.

He endured great risk, shouldered great responsibility, adapted to new situations, easily shared the spotlight, willingly served in support roles, and encouraged everyone. He recovered Paul and brought him to Antioch to minister. He journeyed with him to Cyprus and modern-day Turkey. He was a gospel-shaped servant leader and a grace-giver to the end.

Even in separation from Paul, Barnabas was motivated not by competition but by grace. He desired to redeem and reclaim his nephew, John Mark. Though Paul had reasonable doubts, Barnabas was willing to take the risk of restoring John Mark.

In the gospel, our typical surface fears are resolved. Surface anxieties, like how to pay bills or provide for our needs, are undergirded by God's promise of provision. A gospel identity is free to be relationally and materially generous. This is why Jesus told His followers to consider the flowers and birds, and how God adorns and cares for them (see Luke 12:22–32). Jesus calms our fears, resolves our anxieties, and says "stand up."

The gospel calls us home from failure.

The gospel lifts ours heads in hardship.

The gospel gives solid ground in seasons of fear.

How does the gospel handle our desire for significance? We'll discover that next.

"I came that they may have life
and have it abundantly."

JOHN 10:10

Chapter 12

EMBRACE SMALLNESS

A Gospel Identity Grows Resilience

"He must increase, but I must decrease."

JOHN THE BAPTIST, SPEAKING OF JESUS IN JOHN 3:30

OUR WARNER BROS. STUDIO TOUR was ending. After an informative journey through prop warehouses, backlot facades, and sound stages, we rounded a corner of the walking portion of the tour. The set before us appeared to be the home of Bilbo Baggins from *The Lord of the Rings* movies.[1] But something was off. The furniture was oversized and out of alignment, the dining table and chairs were offset. The awkward display was designed to reproduce one of Hollywood's easiest special effects—forced perspective.

As my wife and I stepped into the display, her seat was closer to the camera and mine farther away. When we pretended to be sitting face-to-face, an image appeared on the screens that made a group of friends immediately burst into unrestrained laughter. Cameras came out, and we looked at each other like, *Uh-oh, what have we done?*

I'll never forget the horror on Dana's face when she saw the image. Suffice to say, I looked like her Hobbit friend and she . . . well, I'm pretty sure I don't want to go there. She immediately made the entire group sign nondisclosure agreements. Then we switched places, and the image reversed—her appearing tiny and me appearing like an out-of-proportion giant. For some reason, she was comfortable sharing the second image.

Forced perspective is a filmmaker's way of deceptively reproportioning things for the viewer. By reordering items or people in proximity to the camera lens, small can look big and vice versa. The distorted view messes with your mind.

Similarly, the world forces perspective on our psyches—skewing our vision of life and what it means to live large or small. Weak identity upsizes the petty and downsizes the valuable, while a gospel identity corrects the distorted view for a rightly proportioned value system.

God's story for you is filled with large blessings, wonderful beauty, and mind-blowing delight found in the least expected of places, and the gospel empowers you to value what He values, even when the world would not.

Have you fallen prey to the world's forced perspective? Let's discover how the gospel corrects our view.

• • •

It was his fourth day of walking alone, plenty of time to wonder why. He walked with very little information. The hills of Samaria were behind him, and he was finally breathing the cooler Mediterranean air. The journey from Samaria to Gaza was more than a hundred miles, most of it downhill, all of it dry and dusty. He didn't know where he was headed, only that God's messenger told him to go south.

Philip, Jesus' disciple, had embarked on the second of two unusual missions. His behavior didn't make sense. After Jesus' ascension, Philip stayed in Jerusalem as the new church grew. But Jesus' followers began to experience persecution from an angry Pharisee named Saul. As the suffering grew, Christians were forced to flee for safety, scattering in every direction and taking the gospel with them.

Of all the places an Israelite would go from Jerusalem, directly north was *not* one of them. The road north led to Samaria, a region of half-Jewish people who were despised by Jews. But Jesus instructed the disciples to take the gospel there, even as He had two years prior. Philip answered that call and moved to Samaria.

If culture defined Philip, he wouldn't have crossed the street to help a Samaritan. But the gospel rearranged his values, broke through his cultural categories, and grew genuine love for all people, including Samaritans. After all, he had been there before with Jesus when the woman at the well became a missionary and helped many in her city meet Jesus.

Philip's story is found in Acts 8. Many Samaritans became believers. In fact, the entire city was joyful because of Philip's teaching. You might say Philip became *somebody* in Samaria. He rose to prominence as the city marveled at his message and miracles. Influential people were drawn, and the number of new believers grew so rapidly that eventually Peter and John journeyed north from Jerusalem to observe the church. In modern terms, Philip experienced smashing success. A traditional identity rooted in "getting the job done for Jesus" or "building something great for God" would have considered this evidence of flourishing.

As grateful as he probably was, Philip didn't allow his ministry results to define him. How do we know? First, because he went *to* Samaria, and second, because he *left* for a long walk south, without knowing why.

The road to Gaza stretched before him for miles. With every step, gravel crunched under his leather sandals. His mind affectionately recalled Samaritan new believers he had grown to love. I wonder if the irony of the situation struck him. In a gospel identity, one day may be flourishing in companionship, and the next can be a long walk alone.

He left behind stunning success, but seemingly lost no sense of significance. Clearly, his identity was not in being "big" versus "small," but in responding to God rather than second-guessing Him—on-mission versus off-mission. Externals did not hold Philip's identity. A person can't be any "bigger" or more significant than to be on mission with his God.

Though Philip walked south with little information, he had no less security or purpose. How? Clearly, his security was not in future plans or insurance policies. His security was in the promises of Jesus. A person can't be any more held together than to be held in the hand of the One who holds it all.

Philip's sense of self was not found in being Jewish, male, good, accomplished, or any other of dozens of identity factors. His sense of self was grounded in His assignment from his Savior. A person can't have a greater purpose than to be aligned with the passion of God.

Walk south. So he did.

He didn't put God on trial or defend the fruitfulness of his work in Samaria. He didn't debate the greener, cooler climate of the Samaritan hills versus the hotter, barren southern desert.

He simply obeyed. What made him capable of such radical but peaceful personal upheaval? What made him willing to leave remarkable significance and productivity?

He was defined by Jesus, not by weak identity factors.

He walked a steady pace, gradually approaching a slow-moving entourage. Drawing closer, he could see a chariot at the center, which made him curious. *Somebody wealthy or powerful, apparently.* As the gap closed, Philip moved to the opposite side of the road and quickened his pace slightly. The contingency with this chariot appeared formidable, and he wanted it clear that he was no threat. As he passed, something caught his ear. Familiar language, foreign accent.

Isaiah! The man in the chariot is reading the prophet aloud.

Then God gave Philip his next instructions. That's how He often does it. He gives obedient followers their next step *when it's time,* little more and rarely before.

"Go over and join this chariot," said the Spirit to Philip (Acts 8:29).

Responding quickly, Philip shouted to the man as he jogged across the road, "Do you understand what you are reading?"

"I have a business degree, but I still need someone to help me with Scripture!" (see vv. 30–31). Frustration was evident in his response. The Ethiopian, an African man and honest seeker of God, had been turned away from worshiping God at the temple in Jerusalem due to religious laws prohibiting a eunuch from entering the Temple. Returning home discouraged, he remained desperate for a relationship with God.

The gospel always reaches for the person religion rejects. Gospel-shaped believers are the arms He uses to do His reaching.

This man was the CFO of Ethiopia, second only to the queen.

Yet material security had not secured his soul. Eagerly, he beckoned for Philip to join him, and together they studied the story of the gospel from the Old Testament, starting with Isaiah 53. That day, the Ethiopian professed his belief in Jesus and was baptized. Then, God's Spirit took Philip far north, and Scripture closes the Ethiopian's story saying he went back home celebrating.

Philip's story doesn't end there. God led him up the Mediterranean coast of Israel, preaching the gospel until he reached the Roman city of Caesarea, where he faithfully served for more than twenty-five years. He later hosted Paul and his entourage of church leaders from Gentile churches all over the Greco-Roman world.

What the gospel did to Philip and others, it will do to us as well—if we allow it to.

WHAT CAN WE LEARN FROM PHILIP'S STORY?

The gospel fills our hearts with unconditional love and erases cultural prejudice.

The fact that Philip went to Samaria is a gospel wonder. He ministered to people who were predispositioned to scorn him. He was relationally under water from day one and would have exhibited uncommon grace and love. He would have absorbed mistreatment and distrust.

Later in Acts 10, though Philip was already there, Jesus led Peter to Caesarea for the express purpose of leading Cornelius's Gentile family to Jesus. Why? Because Peter needed to apply the gospel to his cultural understanding. His Jewishness was too powerful a defining factor in his heart. Even as a church leader, he had security struggles related to his old self. In duplicity, he was torn between pleasing his Jewish Christian friends and accepting his new Gentile Christian friends at the same time (Gal. 2:7–14).

Peter is another reminder that a gospel identity takes shape over a long time as God patiently exposes our insecurities or prejudices and pries our hearts from the grip of weaker defining factors.

Jews despised Gentiles. In a first-century Jewish mind, there were only two groups of people on the planet—Jews and Gentiles. They presumed God loved Jews and rejected Gentiles. It was that stark of a contrast. But the gospel breaks through these man-made ethnic barriers. It tears down racial and cultural differences today, bringing together diverse people as one new race (brothers and sisters, ethnic origin irrelevant; see Eph. 2:11–19).

Philip's story shows us how a gospel identity diffuses cultural tension. Ethnic and cultural factors stop defining us as the gospel definition overpowers and reorders all others. Jesus enables us to love anyone in light of how much we are loved. Throughout history, wherever the *true gospel* is preached, racial tension melts into familial and missional love and unity.

Every day, I serve a church family that is incredibly diverse, not because we planned it, but because that's what the gospel creates. The gospel grows one family worshiping one Savior with one mission and one amazing future. The gospel makes the *heart* of a person more valuable than *ethnicity*. It takes a diverse group of flawed people and makes them so full of love that their surface differences melt into deep friendships. The DNA of gospel identity makes very diverse people strong enough and humble enough to truly love each other. Paul explained that Jesus died "that he might create in himself one new man in place of the two, so making peace, and might reconcile us both to God in one body through the cross, thereby killing the hostility" (Eph. 2:15–16).

The gospel overpowers horizontal significance with vertical significance.

Philip left many for one. He left big ministry for no ministry and one-on-one ministry. How often the world teaches us to do otherwise. In a culture of "upward mobility," we are taught to seek bigger and better—to attach great significance to things of little value. We're taught to construct big boats of balsa wood.

Passion, hard work, and vision are twisted by forced perspective unless the gospel shapes them. In the gospel, significance has been conferred upon us, so we don't need to seek it. This is a fundamental reorientation of living *from* significance rather than *for* it. Our work flows *from* meaning rather than *for* it. This not only changes *why* we work, but *how* we work, and whether we have the courage and trust to submit our work to the leadership and defining love of Jesus.

The gospel brings eternal perspective and defines success by obedience.

In the gospel, obedience is success, and success is obedience. Obedience is my choice. Results, outcomes, and consequences are God's. And a gospel identity allows my heart to be at peace in His assignment and experiencing His results, even if others resist, dismiss, or disagree with His plan.

What would happen if God disrupted your plans as He did with Philip? What if God said, "Walk away"? How deeply are you defined by your stuff or clinging to a comfort zone? God's gifts and blessings should be faithfully managed, but the gospel prevents them from becoming identity factors or anchor points.

Intuitively we tie our hearts to visible things, and when God says "Go," all the anchor points are exposed. Our fear, anxiety, and negotiation with God reveals that, though we love Him, we are weakly grounded in other things. What is it that you could never lose to Jesus? That is where your heart is actually anchored. When a gospel identity is your strongest anchor, you realize, since you can never lose Jesus, you can lose everything else without losing your *self*.

We can't bear for God to untie our anchor points. We *love* Him but don't *know* Him well enough to *trust* Him. In love, He intentionally exposes this flawed identity. Our obedience struggles reveal trust struggles, which expose our fragility. Our rationalization and efforts to preserve the comfort zone reveal our deeper vulnerability. By grace, God releases our grip on weak things to help us experience the strong hold of Jesus.

Remember Chad's fear in the lazy river? We become like him—clinging, kicking, treading water rather than standing in gospel strength.

From his gospel identity, Philip willingly embraced smallness, gladly entered providential transitions, voluntarily loved the unlovely, and reduced himself in obedience to his Savior. His behavior reveals profound authenticity and humble *resilience* in the gospel. He has an accurate sense of both himself and his Savior.

What if God told you to surrender success? What if He called you to leave something large to embrace something small? What if He asked you to reduce your life so that He could enlarge His life in and through you? And what if He never showed you a "large outcome" in this life? When the gospel defines you well, obedience to Him is the highest validator in life. His will, His assignment, and His results are enough.

Irenaeus, a second-century church pastor, tells us that the Ethiopian eunuch became a missionary and spent his life giving the gospel to Ethiopia.[2] It is likely that Philip never knew the fruit of his trip to Gaza. Imagine that. God reduced Philip to enlarge the gospel. Philip trusted Him, and here we are studying the story two thousand years later.

The gospel will grow your heart with this kind of trust. It will let you float with confidence, knowing that Jesus will anchor you. Finding and flourishing in a new self ultimately makes losing the old self worth it. This is why faithful believers who have gone through deep hardship usually say, "I wouldn't ask for it, but I wouldn't trade it."

The gospel makes us secure everywhere and anywhere.

Philip was secure wherever the gospel led him. He was at home wherever Jesus placed Him. In Jerusalem he was a quiet, backstage disciple. In Samaria, he was a senior pastor of a megachurch. On the road to Gaza, he walked in obscurity. With the CFO of Ethiopia, he befriended international wealth. In Caesarea, he loved Greeks and Romans. In every place, he was secure with a psyche that wasn't built on circumstances, but rather on his relationship with Jesus.

Philip's story reminds me of my friend Don Sisk, who has served the Lord all over the world for more than sixty-five years. Don has traveled more than five million miles on Delta Airlines alone, preaching the gospel and encouraging God's servants.

Not long ago, I asked Don, "Are you going to be home soon?"

His response struck me with the stability of his gospel identity. He smiled, laughed, and said, "Home is wherever I am."

And he meant it.

**The gospel gives priority to providential appointments
over personal ambitions.**

Where did Philip *want* to be? My sense is he wanted to be wherever Jesus placed him. His real home was in a new kingdom, and this reality so transformed him that he was driven more by providence than personal ambition. He was resilient enough to be anywhere God placed him. How I wish I had his resilience eight years ago in my seasons of loss.

Though he was a long time in Jerusalem and Caesarea, he was not averse to transition. Though he was briefly in Samaria and the Mediterranean Coast, he wasn't flighty or discontented. For a season he served in large ministry, but he wasn't ego-driven. Then he served in a desert with one, but not because he preferred "small, more authentic ministry." He went where Jesus sent him, and his identity wasn't formed by horizontal elements or opinions. Divine directives trumped personal ambitions or the influential opinions of others. His heart was clearly aligned with gospel values.

His core ambition and deepest value were locked into who Jesus made him, where Jesus placed him. As Chad eventually experienced, no matter where God's Spirit took him, Philip wasn't merely floating from place to place trying to find himself. He was always tracking along solid gospel ground while the river of God's providence took him into each new assignment.

I marvel at Philip's resilience and security. I want it. If we could bottle it like orange juice, I would drink it for breakfast every morning.

The gospel gives eternal purpose to insufficient people.

The stories of Jesus' first followers may give you the idea that they were superhuman, exceptionally gifted, naturally audacious people.

You may be thinking, *I'm no Peter, John, or Philip.* Well, neither were they, in the sense you imagine.

As this chapter has taken shape, I've had the privilege to walk in Jerusalem where many of the events took place. For several days I've explored the Old City, sipping coffee, experiencing the culture, and finding unique places to sit and write for a while.

Of course, the city is much different than it was two thousand years ago, but in many ways it's the same. The markets are teeming with people, buying and selling and surviving. Large crowds of pilgrim worshipers of several faiths are coming and going as cultures mesh (or smash) together on this mountain called Moriah.

I can't escape the raw simplicity of it. There was nothing exceptional about these followers of Jesus. They were getting through life like us—messy, broken, and weak. They were not remarkable. We somehow believe that God blesses or uses the *exceptions*, not the *norms*. Then we think, *I'm just a norm; He doesn't need me.* We're wrong. He is the exception, and we are the norms. He doesn't need us, but He wants us.

More than ever, the twenty-first century has led humanity into isolation. The glass screens of our devices replace authentic, face-to-face relationships. Like the Ethiopian, humanity has sequestered itself into lonely deserts of questions and emptiness. More than ever, believers can be like Philip, sent by God's Spirit to those people. The gospel gives us the answers to share, the will to speak, and the open doors to walk through. We merely have to believe that we matter where He has placed us.

Writing this book has been a bare-knuckle fight with my own weakness. I think, *Who am I to write to others about a process I'm limping forward in? Seems like God would have chosen a conqueror to write this, but he put the task into the hands of a struggler.*

In every providential assignment, I've been in over my head, internally wrestling that God chose the wrong guy. But that's the point. He uses weakness. He gets the credit when He uses incapable vessels to execute divine orders.

Philip couldn't take credit for building a strong church in Samaria or for leading the CFO of Ethiopia to Jesus. He was just a regular guy going where God told him to go, doing what God told him to do. Since he was content to be small, God chose to do big things.

The gospel makes you God's person, in God's time, for God's purposes. Your story unfolds into His larger story, and He makes you a conduit of His grace to those in your world. As you follow Him, He infuses your simple, everyday obedience with extraordinary value and outcomes—whether you're passing a class, making a home, starting a career, or leading a corporation. Whatever you do in alignment with God and in obedience to Him bears eternal significance.

Take heart! A gospel identity teaches us that God sees small things—like us—through the lens of big purposes.

The gospel calls us home from failure. The gospel lifts our heads in hardship. The gospel gives solid ground under every insecurity. The gospel makes our hearts resilient.

But how does the gospel enable me to respond to hurt or injustice?

"So neither he who plants nor he who waters is anything, but only God who gives the growth. He who plants and he who waters are one, and each will receive his wages according to his labor. For we are God's fellow workers. You are God's field, God's building."

1 CORINTHIANS 3:7–9

Chapter 13

BLEED GRACE

A Gospel Identity Makes Peace

"But love your enemies, and do good."

LUKE 6:35

ICE-COLD STARES pierced the thick air of the sandstone room as seventy-one hardened faces glared. These were powerful men—the High Council—responsible for the execution of Jesus, their sights now focused on one of His followers. Stephen's heart was in his throat, but breaking at the same time. The last place he ever imagined standing was before this council, accused of blasphemy, a crime punishable by death.

Stephen had been preaching the gospel in a Jerusalem synagogue, but when the traditionalists unsuccessfully debated his message, they hired professional liars to accuse him. This gave them cause to bring him to trial. Suddenly, Stephen faced a real and potentially fatal possibility.

The biblical account of his story begins early in Acts 6, when the church at Jerusalem descended temporarily into relational conflict. Greek believers and Jewish believers were divided over discrimination in the care of widows. Jewish widows were better cared for than Greek widows, and before long, complaints went viral on Facebook. Gospel identities reverted to ethnic identities, and accusations of prejudice became a problem in the church.

Less secure identities would have swept the conflict under the rug, vented passive-aggressive posts on social media, or polarized the congregation with counter accusations. The situation could have melted down in ugliness, but—to everyone's benefit—some gospel-shaped people decided to be peaceable.

Someone approached the church leaders for resolution. They were similarly approachable and responsive. After hearing the complaints, they led the church family to select seven spiritually mature men to oversee the care of the church family—presumably the first deacons. Stephen was one of the men selected to serve.

This solution accomplished three things. *First*, it allowed the disciples to remain focused on their priorities of prayer and teaching God's Word. *Second*, it allowed other qualified leaders to use their gifts to bless the church. *Third*, it restored unity to the distracted church. As a result, rapid gospel growth returned to the church. It's a story of gospel identity operating in a combustible and emotionally complex situation.

It was shortly after these events that Stephen's preaching led to false accusations and his trial before the Jewish council. What would he say? How would he behave? The tension grows rapidly in Acts 6:15 and forward as Luke writes:

And gazing at him, all who sat in the council saw that his face was like the face of an angel.

And the high priest said, "Are these things so?" And Stephen said:

"Brothers and fathers, hear me." (6:15–7:2)

It's what Stephen didn't say that amazes me. He didn't ask for safety, deliverance, or protection. He didn't fight back or craft a clever defense. He stood with a radiant countenance, full of love, moderated by peace, and operating in confidence. His spirit seemed undisturbed by the bitter, untrue things hurled at him. His heart was not filled with malice or hatred in response. Natural reactions were overcome with gospel responses.

What flowed out of Stephen in hurtful circumstances? The gospel.

He spoke respectfully, "My brothers and honorable fathers, please hear me out . . ." He pleaded compassionately, disregarding danger. His focus was like that of the runner from Marathon—to herald good news to captive hearts. Perhaps he was convinced that they would turn to Christ. Perhaps he knew he was about to go to heaven, and so his gospel values chose to "go out" speaking valuable words: "Your God loves you and wants to redeem you!"

In this grim moment, with the shadow of death looming, Stephen chose to love, and it drops my jaw. Where did this heart come from? How can a man about to be executed show such undying love *for his murderers*?

Stephen's heart reads something like this: "I realize you may kill me . . . this is my one chance to defend myself. If you're going to kill me, please wait long enough to hear me. Before I die, I'd like you to hear why I'm willing to . . ."

The council listened intently as he unfolded the story of God. When he came to Jesus' part in the narrative, he touched a raw nerve, claiming that God couldn't be contained within a man-made temple. This is exactly the wrong thing to say to men whose identity is solely invested into an earthly temple and its associated lucrative religious system.

Stephen explained that God broke out of the temple and became a man—Jesus (Acts 7:48–50). Historically, *temple* is a word denoting the place where God meets man. To the Jews, no place was more sacred. But Jesus redefined the idea of *temple* as He *became* the temple—God with man. In death, Jesus tore down the temple (His body) and raised it again to life (John 2:19), and then He declared in the gospel that God would dwell in the hearts of believers, making every believer the temple of God (see 1 Cor. 3:16–17; 6:19; Eph. 2:21).

In first-century Israel, this was enraging blasphemy. The religious leaders violently exploded and shouted the conversation down. Stephen's message deconstructed centuries-old identity structures, making the leaders feel assaulted as they held more tightly to man-made identity structures than to God.

In anger, they physically dragged Stephen out of Jerusalem and pummeled him with rocks until he was dead.

This was a devastating and discouraging blow to the young church—a game-changing tragedy that could have infused fear and defeat into new believers. But that's not what happened. God turned Stephen's gospel-shaped love into something marvelous. He bled for those who killed him and forgave them with his final breaths—just like Jesus.

IDENTITY BLEEDS

What do we bleed when life cuts us as it did Stephen? What comes out of us when our identity is threatened or hurt? Nothing reveals our true identity more than what comes out of us when our inner world is painfully slashed or trashed. Chances are you've been the victim of someone else's assault, or you will be at some point.

We've already seen that a gospel identity prevents us from being *defined* by hurt. But how does it help us *respond to it*? What does a gospel identity bleed?

It's important to say my thoughts should not minimize or prevent appropriate cooperation with legal authorities in cases of criminality. Regardless of how "the system" should deal with an attack, how will your *heart* deal with it? How will it impact your identity, and what will your soul produce in such times?

The reality is, hurt always *hurts*. Though the stones drew blood and his accusers deserved justice, Stephen's spirit bled something other than victimhood. The injury didn't actually *hurt* him; it just killed him. It took his physical life but not his *psuche* or *zoe* life. The stones transitioned Stephen into God's presence, but they didn't produce typical hatred. Why wasn't he more vindictive? Why wasn't he more self-defensive, demanding justice, fighting for his rights?

He had an inner supply that, when slashed, bled grace and forgiveness.

I *want* this identity. I want a depth of soul that is so well supplied that life's injuries don't diminish the real life within me. The abundant, Spirit-controlled life of a gospel identity simply won't allow life's losses to drive so deep or provoke natural reactions. By contrast, spiritually immature believers fight as the world fights. But mature believers are equipped by the gospel to absorb blows, sow peace, facilitate reconciliation, and spread forgiveness (Matt. 5:9; James 3:18; 2 Cor. 5:19).

A GOSPEL IDENTITY MAKES US PEACEABLE AND GRACIOUS

Stephen and the other leaders in Acts 6 were equipped to deal with relational problems. They were peace*makers*, not merely peace*keepers*, which is why the church family brought the widow issue to them and created a team to resolve problems. They were conflict navigators—resolving complex emotions and leading others toward reconciliation and unity. A gospel identity makes you a peacemaker because, at your core, you have nothing to lose. You become like a doctor who can never catch anything his patients bring to his office. The gospel gives you the spiritual antibodies to be immune to life's worst.

Our reactions to life's intense relational conflicts are powerful indicators of where we find identity. Emotional combustibility can expose weak identity sources. James, eventually the pastor at Jerusalem, wrote that our fleshly fights come more from *within* us than *without*. Our conflicts flow from warring internal desires because we haven't learned to "ask God" for what we need (James 4:1–3). Our fights flare up because we operate from desperate identities demanding that others provide what only God can. The gospel provides another source for our souls. When we receive what we most need from God, there is little reason left to fight with others.

Conflicts often flare up because we are protecting what we fear losing. We react when somebody touches a raw nerve of need, or when we aren't getting what we feel we deserve. When we don't receive these defining things, we grow emotionally thin.

When our weak identities are ruffled, we overreact with anger or self-protection. These acute sensitivities are dead giveaways that something smaller than the gospel defines us.

James's words indicate that our relational conflicts go many layers deep and have more to do with the power and placement of internal desires than the behavior of others. When internal desires define us, we become volatile toward whoever threatens that desire. In every relationship, we choose how to relate—either primarily *giving* or primarily *receiving*. We approach the relationship *from* fullness or *for* it. If we haven't received fullness from Jesus, we expect it from someone else, and become offended when they fail us.

A gospel identity is full enough to *give*, even when not receiving. It is also equipped with great patience and tenderness toward those not operating in a similar gospel identity. Ephesians 4:31–5:2 teaches us to put away bitterness, anger, malice and to bleed tenderness, forgiveness, and love. Following Jesus and walking in love (Eph. 5:1–2) will grow these responses in our hearts.

The most peaceable (and rare) relational environments are those in which everybody is growing and operating out of a strong gospel identity. This is the ideal of a local church community. In these environments, everybody receives because everybody desires to give, and everybody works quickly to resolve conflict with humility, repentance, grace, and forgiveness. The gospel makes us able to lean into problems rather than avoid them, to resolve rather than run from them. It enables us to admit when we are wrong and forgive others when they are. It motivates us to fill hard conversations with peace and grace.

A GOSPEL IDENTITY BLEEDS GRACE

As God called Stephen to bleed, in another sense He calls us to bleed—to be so grounded in Him that we bleed grace in a world that only knows how to bleed shame and rage.

A traditional identity bleeds shame. *If you shame me, I will shame you! If you hit me, I'll hit you.* When facing confrontation or accusation, it bleeds self-defensiveness and fights back. It is bent on winning arguments, not winning hearts. Many traditional identities have been defended at the expense of a more valuable relationship. When winning arguments is more important than winning hearts, we've lost the essence of living out the gospel.

A modern identity bleeds rage. *If you invalidate me, I will invalidate you! Refuse to value what I value, and I will demonize you.* The more our culture embraces modern identity, the more enraged it becomes toward those with differing points of view. Why? Because modern identity deifies its own opinions and then fights to defend them.

A gospel identity bleeds grace. *If you hurt me, I will love and forgive you.* This was Stephen outside Jerusalem as he forgave the stone-throwers.

Injustice is angering. It's easy to hate *hate*. And it doesn't take many days on earth for a person to be hurt. This planet is a brutal place, where sin drives people to damage and dominate each other in unimaginable ways. It only takes about thirty seconds of news coverage to see this on a daily basis.

Amidst this kind of horrific injustice, Stephen was so confident in Jesus, he was able to care deeply even for those who wanted him dead. Just before his death, he proclaimed to his murderers a vision of Jesus standing in heaven. Have you ever wondered why, at the apex of his suffering, he had the fortitude to point out Jesus? I believe he thought they could see what he was seeing. Maybe he expected this hard evidence to change their hearts. He never stopped loving and winning his accusers.

The gospel upsizes God's provision in your life and downsizes others' hurt. It makes you so secure in the *eternal* that you can be resilient with the *temporal*. It makes you so unhurtable that you can absorb hurt, so unoffendable that you can absorb offense without permanent damage. Your soul is re-created of Nerf and wrapped in bubble wrap. Stuff that makes other people crazy with rage and revenge can bounce off or be absorbed.

Honestly, who wouldn't want a Nerf soul?

A more sobering way to say it is that gospel love is *costly love*. Jesus displayed costly love by absorbing the hurt we inflicted upon Him, and He empowers us to display the same costly love toward those who hurt us. We love from positions of such security that we don't experience actual loss when we love so lavishly. Stephen was slandered, misquoted, and maligned. In the face of rage and false accusation, he loved his opposition. He felt this way: "If it comes to losing my life so others might be saved, I choose to lose so someone else can win!" God says to us, "Put on then, as God's chosen ones, holy and beloved, compassionate hearts, kindness, humility, meekness, and patience, bearing with one another and, if one has a complaint against another, forgiving each other; as the Lord has forgiven you, so you also must forgive" (Col. 3:12–13).

Stephen had a choice when things went badly. *Do I defend myself or extend myself? Do I close off or open up? Do I risk being hurt or run for my life?* Because of his eternal security with Jesus, Stephen was full enough to extend and expend himself, no matter the cost.

Gospel identity is the *only* identity that functions this way, and it makes all the relationships of your life able to flourish in serving and selflessness—"through love serve one another" (Gal. 5:13).

Let me share the most powerful modern example of this that I have ever witnessed.

. . .

On September 6, 2018, off-duty Dallas police officer Amber Guyger returned home from a long shift. She was tired and inadvertently parked on the wrong floor of the parking garage attached to her apartment building. On the wrong floor, she approached an apartment she *thought* was hers and noticed the door was open. Immediately concerned, she drew her gun and proceeded into the apartment, anticipating an intruder.[1]

Sitting in what she thought was her living room was an African American man she did not recognize. Panic took over, and tragically, Amber shot and killed the man. His name was Botham Jean, a greathearted, innocent young man with a steadfast faith in Jesus Christ. He was simply sitting in his own apartment that night as his life abruptly ended for no rational reason.

For the next year, the city of Dallas was gripped by this tragedy. The resulting trial became a racially charged media frenzy, sparking daily debate and rage on every side of the issue. The case was complex and emotional. Clearly Amber reacted wrongly, though not maliciously, and people on every side of the issue demanded justice.

As the trial closed, in spite of Amber's profound remorse, she was convicted and sentenced to ten years in prison for second-degree murder. Justice was served, but nobody felt "better." Dozens of lives were pointlessly but permanently disrupted, and it seemed there was no positive outcome. The heart of the city felt deeply for both the Jean and the Guyger families.

Enter the gospel.

Just before Amber was incarcerated, the Jean family was permitted to present their "witness impact statements." The courtroom was emptied of most observers, but the cameras stayed on. The Jean family, all committed to Jesus, was told they could say anything to Amber as long as they didn't issue threats or use profanity.[2] You can imagine, this is the time when victims typically speak their minds and spew their raw hatred.

Those who followed the case waited to hear what the Jean family would say to Botham's murderer. What happened next echoed around the world.

Botham's younger brother, Brandt, quietly stepped to the microphone to speak. He carefully and thoughtfully selected his words and spoke tenderly as he brushed tears from his eyes. When the world expected rage, Brandt bled grace, and the world held its breath.

"I don't even want you to go to jail. . . . I think giving your life to Christ would be the best thing that Botham would want you to do. I love you as a person, and I don't wish anything bad on you."[3]

Brandt paused, looked at the judge, brushed away more tears, and then hesitatingly asked a bizarre question: "Can I give her a hug, please?" There was an awkward pause. "*Please?*"[4] The look on Brandt's face was earnest, as if he were thinking, *Something in me will never be whole if I can't give this lady a hug.*

To everyone's surprise, Amber nodded toward the judge, who then gave approval. As Brandt stepped down from the witness stand, Amber stepped around the defense table and literally ran into Brandt's arms, collapsing in tears as she buried her head into his shoulder. She wept passionately as they embraced for a long time. And the world wept with them.

I watched this video three times in one day—in Dunkin' Donuts, at the DMV, and at home with my wife. All three times, I was a blubbering fool. (I've cried in the DMV before, but usually out of frustration.) How is this possible? Who could imagine a victim embracing a murderer with such boundless grace and compassion? Later I heard the rest of the story.

Not long after Brandt hugged Amber, the judge—Tammy Kemp—stepped out of the courtroom and reentered minutes later. She went over to the Jean family and hugged each one, telling them how sorry she was for their loss.[5] Then she did something that only one other judge (that I know of) has done in the history of time.

She stepped toward the guilty. She crouched down in front of Amber and gave her a Bible, saying, "Read this."[6]

Amber stood, attempting to hug the judge, but the bailiff stepped in. Judge Kemp pulled him back, giving permission. What I saw next has *happened to* me, but I've never seen it with my eyes.

The judge embraced the guilty, and together they wept. Judge Kemp gave Amber the gospel and encouraged her to entrust herself to Jesus. When Amber whispered something in her ear, she replied, "Ma'am, it's not because I am good. It's because I believe in Christ. None of us are worthy."[7]

The gospel is this: The Judge stepped away from the bench; He came to me, the guilty, to embrace me in grace. I have been forgiven. Therefore, I can forgive.

. . .

Stephen's death was a senseless tragedy—a total loss. Or was it? A gospel identity is convicting to those who *witness* it.

As the final stones were hurled at Stephen's head, his body went limp and lifeless. The savage rulers successfully silenced a golden voice. But the gospel gives hope in death. Crucifixion precedes resurrection. Bad circumstances are no match for God's good purposes.

At this very scene, God was using evil deeds to validate gospel grace to a single stubborn soul. The onlooker's face was ice cold, but his heart was subtly conflicted. *Why isn't this man suffering more?* Perhaps he pushed back a nagging thought.

Arms folded, head high, he presided over the scene. Those casting stones did so with his tacit approval. He was among the most prominent and brilliant in the religious hierarchy. He was masterfully educated, culturally versed, and spiritually zealous for God. He had risen to the heights of respect in Jerusalem and beyond, and he hated the followers of Jesus. He vowed to extinguish them and had the authority to rid the world of them.

He was powerful, well backed, and ruthless. He was public enemy number one for the church of Jesus. He watched life leave Stephen's body, expecting a rising tide of fear to seize the followers of Jesus.

I wonder if he expected a strong feeling of superiority and victory to surge through his adrenal glands. Surely he expected to sense the pleasure of God on his zealous religiosity.

Instead he felt something disruptive: conviction, the pricking of his conscience ("it is hard for thee to kick against the pricks"— Acts 9:5 KJV). God was after his heart, which only made him harder and more determined. However, Saul saw something in Stephen that reflected a kind of love he had likely never known.

For all that he despised about Jesus' followers, there was something powerful in them. They seemed to *actually know* God and *experience* His love—a foreign concept for a Pharisee.

One day this man would write: "Love one another with brotherly affection. Outdo one another in showing honor" (Rom. 12:10), and also, "Above all these put on love, which binds everything together in perfect harmony. And let the peace of Christ rule in your hearts" (Col. 3:14–15).

His name was Saul. At Stephen's execution, he was a religious, fire-breathing dragon. No one was more devoted to traditional Judaism. But that's all about to change.

Maybe Stephen entered heaven, saw God's plan, broke into a wide smile, and said, "Ohhh!"

The gospel was about to rock the first-century world.

"And falling to his knees he cried out with a loud voice,
'Lord, do not hold this sin against them.'
And when he had said this, he fell asleep.
And Saul approved of his execution."

ACTS 7:60–8:1

Chapter 14

FALL DOWN

A Gospel Identity Forms in Worship

"The young lions suffer want and hunger;
but those who seek the LORD lack no good thing."

PSALM 34:10

THE DRAGON ARRIVED in Damascus, but the last tendrils of smoke
were lofting upward from his once fire-breathing lungs. Rage was
forcibly suspended. He sat powerless and numb from the events
that befell him. With nothing to eat or drink, he stared into total
blackness for three days, his mind racing and his life a blank canvas.

His assistants checked him into an inn somewhere in the city.
With no appetite and no friends, he waited in silence as instructed.
The wait was agonizing, but also redefining for every category Saul
had in his religiously zealous self. He was not who he thought. God
was not who he thought, and neither was Jesus. Saul had gotten it
all wrong—the entire Old Testament (as we call it today) had come
unraveled during three dark days of deliberation.

A radical, redefining moment had revealed to him an unimaginable horror—he was fighting on the wrong side of a cosmic war and was found opposing the God he claimed to serve.

After Stephen's stoning, Saul had redoubled his religious efforts to brutalize Jesus' followers. Likewise, often our response to failure or spiritual prodding within performance-based systems is to simply try harder. It's a destructive downward spiral. For Saul, to "try harder" had meant to intensify his slaughter. Murder more Christians.

He had been a raging monster, rampaging against innocent people, bloodthirsty to satisfy his insatiable appetite for religious achievement. It's ironic that extreme religiosity transformed Saul into a devourer. He demonized those who loved him, and esteemed those who did not.

Jesus sacrificed Himself to *save* people, but Saul enlarged himself by *consuming* them.

This is the fruit of a weak self on the steroid of high-performance. People are expendable, sacrificed on the altar of an enlarged identity. Relationships become a *means* to constructing or maintaining self rather than the joyful fruit of gospel community. Real, loving, substantive friendships are substituted for those of self-service—mutual usefulness.

His story in Acts 9 shows that every time Saul attempted to stomp out a flicker of the gospel, new sparks scattered and caught fire in every direction. God leveraged Saul's hate to spread grace. Some believers fled northeast to Damascus, and when Saul's intelligence sources reported it, he set out immediately for Syria. When they heard he was coming, they feared for their lives.

The journey to Damascus was 150 miles for Saul and his entourage. On the final day of travel, Saul perhaps could see the city in the distance and began anticipating the satisfaction of arresting the renegades. He probably gloated in how "pleased" he believed God would be with his assistance. A traditional identity often attempts to in-debt God by doing Him favors.

At midday, the sun high, Saul's team stopped along the roadside as he prayed. It was the second of three times daily when a devoted Pharisee would stand piously facing Jerusalem to offer self-righteous prayers. This time was different.

Midsentence, Saul's prayer was dramatically disrupted by a light so bright that it immediately drove him to the ground in fear. He described it as being brighter than the sun, blinding him, and rendering him helpless (Acts 26:13–14).

Saul! The call rocked his soul. He had read of such encounters in Scripture and knew this was a vision of God. His heart melted in the presence of white-hot holiness. He feared for his life as his name was repeated a second time.

"Saul, why are you persecuting me?" (Acts 9:4). The voice thundered with profound force. The incriminating *redefining* question seized his mind. His adrenaline-laced reasoning scrambled for an answer as his nerves spiked. *Who is this? If God, how am I persecuting Him?* Suddenly his self-assurance evaporated. The dragon wilted before his Creator.

Fumbling for words, physically trembling, he asked, "Who are you, Lord?"

It was the question of his life.

Everything hinged on the answer to this one question. True for Saul, true for the woman at the well, and true for us as well. *Who is Lord? Who can speak and flatten me to the ground with His voice? Who can give me a source of living water? Who has ultimate authority to define me?* The question strikes at the core of who I am in light of who has highest power and authority over me.

Saul and men like him had constructed God in their own image and placed Him into a system of performance in which they were successful. They excelled marvelously in this man-made system.

The next words were the last thing Saul expected to hear.

Slowly the voice answered with an authority that comprehensively reconstructed Saul's self in just three words. *I. Am. Jesus.*

This single answer reordered Saul. Everything he believed to be true about himself collapsed on that road. The identity he had worked his entire life to build—a long, obedient childhood, many years of religious education, decades of spiritual devotion—all came undone. In a fraction of a second, he lost everything he had worked to gain in the light of who Jesus is (Phil. 3:7–8).

Like a million-piece jigsaw puzzle that he had forced together in all the wrong ways, every piece of 1,500 years of biblical history came detached and fell into a disjointed pile. Saul and his heritage of religiosity had taken bits and pieces of God's story and glued it all together the wrong way—splinters of truth in God's name, but distorted and perverted and far from His heart (Isa. 29:13).

All the pieces lay in a fragmented pile in Saul's confused psyche. *I. Am. Jesus.* The words reverberated to his core for three days. As he replayed the experience outside of Damascus, one by one, his soul picked up all the puzzle pieces of Scripture and reexamined them through the lens of "I. Am. Jesus."—the gospel. In light of Jesus, they all fit together perfectly and more beautifully than Saul could have ever imagined. The whole of Scripture points to Jesus (see Luke 24:27, 44; John 5:39). A new reality gave way to a new identity.

This was comprehensive re-creation. Everything he thought he was, everything he intended to be and do—all ceased to be. His anchor points crumbled, and as the dust dissipated, there was a person, standing highly exalted, towering over the rubble of Saul's former self—Jesus the Messiah, declaring Himself Lord, God, Creator, and Savior, and laying claim to ultimate authority over Saul.

The implications would require far more than three days to process. This was an identity tsunami, and Saul would spend the rest of his life describing it to others and persuading them to enter the same new life by faith—redeemed, reborn, strengthened, and gradually transformed into the image of Jesus (Col. 1:9–18; Rom. 8:29; Gal. 4:9).

· · ·

I imagine the knock on the door jolted him. Having lost his appetite, he was completely absorbed in surveying his pre-tsunami life. There it is again, a knock—soft, as if the person on the other side is hoping no one will answer. Saul stood and began feeling his way toward the door.

Then it slowly opened. Saul couldn't see him, but a timid, middle-aged man tentatively stepped into the room.

"Are you Saul?"

"Yes, I am." His eyes were covered with thick scales, providentially placed to protect his eyes and force him to reckon with his inward brokenness. How often our external performance is merely a curtain we hide behind, blinding us to God's necessary deeper work.

"I am Ananias. God sent me to you."

Ananias was a follower of Jesus instructed to find Saul—a terrifying command. Jesus assured Ananias that Saul was a new believer prepared for a unique purpose. Like Ananias, God's calling often leads us into precarious situations, but the gospel fortifies us to face them.

Seeing the man's weakness, Ananias's heart softened and fear dissipated. Realizing Saul's blindness, he stepped fully into the room. For a few seconds he stood face-to-face with the man Christians most feared. Surreal. It likely never entered his mind that he would have an opportunity to *love* Saul.

Lesser identities would have seized the opportunity to kill the enemy. But a gospel identity behaves differently toward enemies—and newly repentant brothers.

I imagine a pregnant pause between the two men. Saul, the killer of Jesus-followers, meets Ananias, the Jesus-follower. But God has quenched the flames of the dragon. Ananias looked into Saul's flattened countenance. The mask of fiery rage had fallen, revealing the fragile man hiding within. Nobody had ever seen Saul in this self-emptied, weakened state. Going forward, weak Saul is all the world will ever see (2 Cor. 12:9–10), though he's never quite comfortable being weak. Neither are we. But until we are weak, the gospel can never grow strong in and through us.

Perhaps Ananias's first thought was, *This man was coming to Damascus to kill me.*

But then Ananias, by God's Spirit, had a gospel-shaped thought: *This man is my brother, and now I love him.*

His heart involuntarily enlarged, putting gospel identity brilliantly on display. He raised his arms, not to strike but to bless. He rested his hands on Saul's shoulders, not with force but gentleness. He let out an empathetic sigh, and for the first time, Saul experienced personal love from a Jesus-follower he had intended to kill.

He couldn't see the tears forming in Ananias's softened eyes, but to the core of his soul, he felt the compassion in his voice.

"Brother Saul . . ."

WHAT DOES SAUL'S STORY TEACH US ABOUT GOSPEL IDENTITY?

Saul's story parallels Peter's, and would make an expansive identity study in itself. But let's focus on a few simple applications.

We've explored many ways God leads us through losing, finding, and into flourishing. What we've primarily seen is that *He* is the creator and cultivator of gospel identity. He does the work in us, and He uses providential experiences in our lives to reshape us into Jesus' image.

A gospel identity could well be described as "the best version of you, shaped like Jesus," or perhaps, "Jesus' life and character uniquely shaped like you." It's all of our uniqueness brought to fullness and conformed to the character and calling of Jesus. The gospel takes our God-given design, identity factors, life experiences (positive and negative), and weaves them together in the image of and for the purposes of Jesus. This is the most cohesive and durable life-journey.

Up to now, we've seen essentially five ways God shapes this new identity:

- He calls us to repent in failure.

- He lifts our heads in hardship.

- He stabilizes our fears with solid ground.

- He shows us big value in small things.

- He makes us able to bleed grace.

Many of the things God uses to shape our identity are *involuntary*. It's our response that is *voluntary*. Saul humbled himself and submitted to God's redefining work. He *fell down* before Jesus and *allowed* the comprehensive re-creation of his identity. He placed faith in Jesus—both for salvation and for formation. For the rest of his life, he embraced his new self, believing Jesus, and pressing toward spiritual maturity. He described it this way in Philippians 3:7–14:

> But whatever gain I had, I counted as loss for the sake of Christ. Indeed, I count everything as loss because of the surpassing worth of knowing Christ Jesus my Lord. For his sake I have suffered the loss of all things and count them as rubbish, in order that I may gain Christ and be found in him, not having a righteousness of my own that comes from the law, but that which comes through faith in Christ, the righteousness from God that depends on faith—that I may know him and the power of his resurrection, and may share his sufferings, becoming like him in his death, that by any means possible I may attain the resurrection from the dead.
>
> Not that I have already obtained this or am already perfect, but I press on to make it my own, because Christ Jesus has made me his own. Brothers, I do not consider that I have made it my own. But one thing I do: forgetting what lies behind and straining forward to what lies ahead, I press on toward the goal for the prize of the upward call of God in Christ Jesus.

A gospel identity takes shape in basically two ways—first by *experience* and second by *cultivation*. How can we participate in God's process? He does the work, but He invites us to *cultivate*—to engage our hearts in it. We can't produce the transformation, but we can avail ourselves of the resources He provides (James 1:2–4; Col. 3:15–16).

In this and the next chapter, let's broadly examine three ways we can cultivate new selves.

A GOSPEL IDENTITY GROWS THROUGH AUTHENTIC WORSHIP

Jesus' presence is the most powerful reshaping force in life—as it was for the disciples and Saul. A key to growing a gospel identity is to practice His presence. The gospel invites us to enter into His presence of our own volition (Heb. 4:16). Over and over the Psalms invite us to make God our ultimate reference point:

> Serve the LORD with gladness!
> Come into his presence with singing!

> Know that the LORD, he is God!
> > It is he who made us, and we are his;
> > we are his people, and the sheep of his pasture.

> Enter his gates with thanksgiving,
> > and his courts with praise! (Ps. 100:2–4)

> Those who look to him are radiant,
> > and their faces shall never be ashamed. . . .

> Oh, taste and see that the LORD is good!
> > Blessed is the man who takes refuge in him!
> Oh, fear the LORD, you his saints,
> > for those who fear him have no lack! . . .

> The LORD redeems the life of his servants;
> > none of those who take refuge in him will be
> > condemned. (Ps. 34:5, 8–9, 22)

Think of *looking* on Jesus and *becoming* radiant. You can try to "glow for God" and fail, or you could simply look long enough for radiance to materialize unpretentiously. This is how falling before Jesus in worship, prayer, confession, and submission is so transformational. A gospel identity glows as we voluntarily celebrate Him, remember Him, and continually reset our hearts in light of the gospel. Every moment, we can choose to make Him our reference point.

Every spiritual practice is designed to bring us into His presence and immerse our hearts in the gospel to be shaped by His grace. This is why gathering and worshiping with believers in a biblical local church is vital. It's why consistent personal time with Jesus in His Word is powerful. It's why commemorating the Lord's Table and personal prayer is so significant as our hearts return to the cross and experience the resetting realities of the gospel.

This is why a gospel identity does not simply form by checking off a list of religious tasks. Religion *structures* us; the gospel *captivates* us. This identity only forms as we enter His presence and *experience* Jesus personally and relationally.

As winter comes to New England, I could look at a photo of a fire all day long and yet never enjoy warmth. But if I stand in the presence of a fire, warmth is unavoidable. So, a gospel identity forms as I enter His presence and *encounter* His trustworthiness day by day all the way home. Religion says, "Do for God. Live up to God," but the gospel says first, "Be with Him."

Saul's experience brought him into redefining proximity to Jesus and truth. But it took him the rest of his life and many more God-ordained encounters for the infinite reality to unfold in and through him.

GOD REASSURES GOSPEL IDENTITY OVER AND OVER

The Damascus road, as redefining as it was, was only one of many times God strengthened or reaffirmed Saul's identity. He shared at least four other times in his journey when God did a similar work.

The first was as Saul began ministry in the thriving Greco-Roman trading hub of Corinth. He arrived in Corinth on his second journey and was not in a good place. He had been relentlessly persecuted and traumatized by enemies. He had been arrested, falsely accused, beaten or stoned, and driven away on multiple occasions. He had narrowly escaped death numerous times and had been alone for many months—something always discouraging for Saul (now called Paul to identify with his Gentile audience). He was forced to flee from Berea in Northern Greece and ended up in the city of Athens, a city overtaken in idolatry and pagan philosophy. In Athens, he was alone, low on resources, and spent of energy, but nonetheless compelled to share the gospel. His time there bore more ridicule than fruit, and finally God's providence moved him west to nearby Corinth (Acts 17 and 18).

As Paul arrived in Corinth, he was weak and depleted (1 Cor. 2:3; Acts 18); and he was out of money, requiring him to take a tent-making job, reducing his ministry to one day a week. And he was alone, rendering him discouraged and timid. He was probably worried about the churches he had planted and the friends he had left behind. When his companions Timothy and Silas finally arrived, his spirit was immediately revived, and his resources were replenished, allowing him to resume full-time gospel ministry.

For all the hardship that preceded it, his eighteen months on this beautiful, sloping shore of the Ionian Sea proved to be some of his best and most fruitful. The church at Corinth blossomed, his friends were reunited, his employers—Aquila and Priscilla—became longtime gospel partners, and he wrote his famous letter to the church at Rome. Things were good, for the time being.

Paul was likely dealing with a form of PTSD. He was waiting for the other shoe to drop—*At what point will the opposition begin? Will I get beaten or stoned? When will this go badly? Will I flee or lose my life?*

In the midst of these fears and doubts, his friend Luke described God's assurance this way: "And the Lord said to Paul one night in a vision, 'Do not be afraid, but go on speaking and do not be silent, for I am with you, and no one will attack you to harm you, for I have many in this city who are my people.' And he stayed a year and six months, teaching the word of God among them" (Acts 18:9–11). God doesn't show up to calm fears that don't exist. Paul clearly needed to encounter God's reality again, and God was gracious to settle Paul's fears.

Similar experiences happened time and again. Every time he faced fear, discouragement, or uncertainty, God somehow reminded him of his true identity. It happened after a riot, arrest, and beating in Jerusalem (Acts 23:11); in the middle of a terrifying hurricane at sea (Acts 27:23–24); and again in Rome when he stood alone pleading his case (2 Tim. 4:16–17).

God never left Paul alone, and He will never leave you alone. God never took issue with Paul's fears or doubts, but rather ministered to and resolved them with His grace. Time after time, He allowed Paul to reexperience His presence and trustworthiness.

We cultivate a gospel identity first through authentic worship—falling before Jesus, remembering *who* He is and *what* He has done and *who* that makes us. At our weakest, He is always ready to stabilize us again.

As you move from *losing* to *finding* to *flourishing,* there are two more big ways you can cultivate your gospel identity. Let's find out what they are on this last step of our journey.

"O Lord of hosts, blessed is the one
who trusts in you!"

PSALM 84:12

Chapter 15

GROW FORWARD

A Gospel Identity Forms through Patient Cultivation

"So we do not lose heart. Though our
outer self is wasting away, our inner self
is being renewed day by day."

2 CORINTHIANS 4:16

MY STRUGGLE has persistently resided between *knowing* the gospel on one hand and *experiencing* it on the other. Moving it from my head to my heart is a daily necessity, and it is God's carefully orchestrated loss in my life that has most activated gospel growth. He has gently deconstructed my weak identities (and still is) and has patiently shown me over and over His truer definition.

My temptation is to be embarrassed over the piles of weak identity fragments strewn on life's pathway behind me, but it's a reality for every growing Christian. This is the normal journey for believers. This is what we all "signed up for" when we placed our faith in Jesus. We build with weak things. Then Jesus lovingly breaks us down, and the gospel rebuilds us with grace. If there are no piles of weak identities in your past, then you're either not growing, or you're a very new believer. There will be. Eventually you will thank God for His gentle sledgehammer of truth and the new-creature-work He does in your life. He tears down weak identities in all of us, and any embarrassment or attempt to hide merely reveals another one soon to fall.

The gospel makes the process something you can rejoice in. "I will boast all the more gladly of my weaknesses, so that the power of Christ may rest upon me" (2 Cor. 12:9).

In my deep loss, truths I had been taught all of my life were forced from the backstage into the spotlight of verity. Is it *really true*? Am I only what I do? Am I merely a producer—the sum of all these surface definitions—or is there something truer and more defining underneath this glued-together pile of weakness? Will the gospel actually come through? Can it hold me together? Will I experience Paul's reality from 2 Corinthians 12:10, "For the sake of Christ, then, I am content with weaknesses, insults, hardships, persecutions, and calamities. For when I am weak, then I am strong"? Does God truly take delight in my brokenness and prove Himself when I have nothing to offer Him or others?

Will I actually find anything in this loss?

I repeatedly forget what the gospel makes truest about me. It's a natural drift. My weak heart is easily drawn from vertical back toward horizontal identity in pursuit of weak validation and flimsy security. We all naturally seek *affirming* love from others, *security* from material things, and *significance* in our personal performance. This is the natural force of gravity of a horizontal-identity world. It can frame our Christian journey through "what we do for Him." We subconsciously drift from "what Jesus has done for us," gradually sliding from grace to works.

If our orientation is *gospel*, then we live fully out of what Jesus has done for us. The journey remains one of grace and fullness. We live as beloved children (Eph. 5:1); and our identities remain rooted in His acceptance, security, and significance.

If our orientation is *works*, then God's grace grows smaller, our performance larger, and our sense of *who we are* begins to flow from what we do for God—always an exit ramp from the gospel journey. We turn Jesus into a traditional identity—on our good days feeling loved and on our bad days feeling rejected. We move from living out of *who Jesus says we are* to living up to *who Jesus demands that we be*. It's a subtle shift, but it drains the joy and life from the journey of knowing Jesus, and it makes the Christian life very discouraging.

A gospel identity is life-giving; a temporal identity is life-draining. *Trying* to be my best self is discouraging and regretful. *Growing* into who Jesus says I am is energizing and joyful.

Oh, the contrast! On the surface, the terms, verses, and theological ideas can sound identical. The lingo is similar, the externals may appear the same, but the actual *experiences* are polar opposites.

GROW IN GRACE

We are conditioned to think of identity as something we achieve. But we cannot think of gospel identity in this way. When we do, we immediately reduce it to a traditional identity with merely a gospel label. This inevitably inflates us in pride or deflates us in failure. We intuitively try to measure progress against some measuring stick, even if we create the stick ourselves. But a gospel identity must resist these old-self instincts.

We have to think of gospel identity as already achieved and organically coming into view, like a tree that grows in healthy conditions. We don't manufacture it; He manifests it. We don't force or fake it; He grows it. It's a product of *trust* more than *try*, *rest* more than *effort*. It materializes from organic processes rather than mechanical ones.

Larry didn't *try* to be my son. He was my son. He heard my heart and trusted my words. He rested in my presence. He believed me. It's that simple. His *belief* is what produced his new experience of restfulness.

As with all identity processes, the growth of a gospel identity happens more subconsciously than consciously—which makes the cultivation of our internal thoughts and conversations so pivotal to the process.

Consider how the tree in Psalm 1 is growing deep roots in rich soil (meditating on God's Word day and night), or how Chad was led to stand up on solid ground. As Peter was invited to "feed my lambs" and "fish for men," or Philip was invited to downsize himself in obedient faith, or Ananias was invited to love his enemy in risky faith—gospel identity is something we *receive* by faith and *develop* by acting or operating in faith. It materializes into reality as we engage and experience God at work (Heb. 11:6). As we learn to view our life experiences through a gospel lens, a new understanding takes shape, producing new behaviors.

We will spend the rest of our lives daily navigating away from old-self tendencies and "growing up" into who we already are in

Jesus. We can't create it, but we can cultivate it. And we certainly can't measure it. We must live in the faith-based confidence of Philippians 1:6—that Jesus began and is continuing His good work in us until we see Him. Every attempt to measure progress puts the focus on us instead of Jesus—inevitably drawing us into a comparison game. This is never a gospel practice, as Paul taught the Corinthians, saying, "Not that we dare to classify or compare ourselves. . . . when they measure themselves by one another and compare themselves with one another, they are without understanding" (2 Cor. 10:12).

It's the fruit you can't measure that most evidences your gospel identity and most glorifies God. It's the transformation you didn't force that most reveals Jesus alive in you. It's the results you can't post on social media—the fruit you won't see until heaven—that most defines your fruitfulness in God's economy. It's the growth you didn't see that is most evidential of real gospel transformation.

Until then, we patiently tend the garden of our hearts and faithfully devote ourselves to worshiping and walking with Jesus. Gospel identity is a by-product of experiencing a real relationship with Jesus through His Word.

A GOSPEL IDENTITY GROWS AS WE ENGAGE IN LOVING SERVICE TO JESUS AND OTHERS

Serving Jesus and others is like stretching and exercising new gospel muscles. It's living out who you really are—putting the gospel into practice. Without stretching and using your gospel identity, it will atrophy, and you will continually forget who you are (2 Peter 1:9). You will stagnate rather than flourish.

With Jesus, Paul instinctively asked two defining questions—
Who are You? and *What do You want me to do?* He became defined
by "who Jesus is," and that definition naturally asked, "Why am
I here?" A *much-loved* soul desires to *love back* with obedience.
A full heart asks, "How do I follow this Savior and lead others to
Him?" We can't help but actively love Him once we experience
how much He loves us (1 John 4:19). The gospel motivates the
heart to love, and loving God motivates the heart to trust Him
and obey Him (John 14:15; 15:10).

New Testament believers experienced that "Ohhh . . ." that
caused them to live out the gospel. They loved, served, gave, and
expended willingly. Their new identities moved from their *heads*
to their *hearts* to their *hands*. They *wanted* to fall before Jesus in
worship, and *wanted* to live like Him in service and self-sacrifice.

Peter, Paul, and John later penned letters of instruction to believers, and they always described God's love before they delivered God's directives. They explained the gospel as the source of
all loving and doing for Jesus. Why? Because as the gospel saves
us it also motivates and enables us. It produces behavior modeled
after Jesus. Paul wrote, "For it is God who works in you, both to
will and to work for his good pleasure" (Phil. 2:13).

In the gospel, *doing* flows from *loving*, and *loving* from *being loved*.

This is how gospel identity becomes a fountainhead of fruitfulness. It's not a name badge you wear. It's a reality you live out of.
It creates and drives new sets of desires, new affections, and new
behaviors. It is reminded every day of who Jesus is, who we are,
and what He has called us to do.

Ananias *loved* the man who was coming to *kill* him. Only the
gospel enabled him to love himself appropriately and love Saul

selflessly at the same time. Jesus said this kind of unearthly love is what most proves the gospel to others. "By this all people will know that you are my disciples, if you have love for one another" (John 13:35).

By grace, Ananias processed fear, risk, and criticism and was able to minister to Saul. A gospel identity supplied him with all the grace needed to face impossible circumstances with radical open-heartedness. The key to extending such lavish grace is to understand and experience the supply we've been given.

I illustrated this to our church by inviting one of our pastors to the platform. I handed him a large jar with four small M&M's in it. When I asked him to share, he found it difficult. There were precious few chocolate candies, and his thinking was, *I'd better keep these for myself!* The congregation identified with his sentiment.

It's hard to give away what you have precious little of. Isn't this why we struggle so much with the risk of being hurt, giving ourselves away, or living generously? We live with such thin margins that we don't have the emotional or spiritual reserves to live as lavishly as first-century believers.

The psychology of the illustration changed when I pulled out several party-sized bags of M&M's. With reckless abandon, I ripped the bags open and dumped them haphazardly into the empty jar. M&M's flowed like a river into the jar and out onto the floor. The congregation laughed hysterically as candy-covered chocolates inundated a Sunday morning message.

After the chaos, I said, "Hey, can I have some M&M's?"

Now immersed in more M&M's than any human should eat in several years, his response brought another round of laughter: "Yes, please! Help yourself. I could never eat all these."

What changed? What made his psyche willing? *Forcing* him to share his original four M&M's wouldn't have changed his heart. Commanding him to be joyful wouldn't have changed his heart. He may have begrudgingly complied, but what brought about the *authentic change of heart?* This organic transformation is what we seek—not merely a forced compliance but real newness. A gospel identity materializes as we sense, *This really is me now. It wasn't before, but God has changed me.*

Being lavished with candies makes it easy to give them away. Abundance changes things. Sounds like Jesus when He says, "I came that they may have life and have it abundantly" (John 10:10).

A gospel identity immerses you in abundance. We have been graced with so much life, we can give it away lavishly. We are so tightly secured that we can freely distribute grace and never run out. This is to live from overflow, so blessed that we freely bless others.

Jesus described it this way: "Whoever believes in me, as the Scripture has said, 'Out of his heart will flow rivers of living water'" (John 7:37–38).

Oswald Chambers comments, "If you believe in Jesus, you will find that God has nourished in you mighty torrents of blessing for others."[1] "Keep right at the Source, and—you will be blessed personally? No, out of you will flow rivers of living water, irrepressible life. We are to be centres through which Jesus can flow as rivers of living water in blessing to every one."[2]

It's what Psalm 1 defines as a tree being planted by a river. A healthy tree can endure every season, the battering of every kind of storm and stress, because its roots run deep, connected to an unending, internal supply that makes it externally flourishing. This tree is perpetually durable and inevitably fruitful.

Like Ananias, because of *whose* you are, *who* you are, and *why* you are, you have an internal supply of all the resources you will ever need, given to you to give away. You're the child of a gracious Father who has given you permission to give your life away because His life supply will never run dry.

A GOSPEL IDENTITY GROWS THROUGH A LIFETIME OF PATIENT CULTIVATION

Do you remember sitting in the back seat of the car on a long journey asking your parents, "Are we there yet?" We will never *feel* there until we actually are there. Until then, we must settle in for a long road, faithfully nurturing our souls in God's truth. J. I. Packer said, "Our spiritual life is at best a fragile convalescence, easily disrupted."[3]

The pace can be frustrating, but God is in no hurry, and He's always forming you. Jesus spent all of His earthly life walking— three miles per hour—everywhere He went. Nine weeks each year, He was either walking ninety miles toward Jerusalem, celebrating in the city for a week, or walking back home. This was the schedule God constructed to ensure that Israel's life was worship-paced with Him as center. He similarly desires to be the center of your attention and life-pace.

The story of Jesus' followers continues to unfold far beyond the scope of this book. They continued throughout their lives to struggle in their new identities. Old-self tendencies, and seasons of discouragement were common but not defining. Their weaknesses were real, but they continued to submit them to Jesus. Paul struggled with a flagrant personality (Acts 23:2–5). Peter struggled with racial bias (Gal. 2:11–17). Barnabas and Saul had their irreconcilable perspectives (Acts 15:36–41; 2 Tim. 4:11). New churches struggled to be unified, to mesh cultures, and to stay on mission. The New Testament is filled with instruction that essentially says, *This is who Jesus is, this is who you are, and this is what that looks like.*

We shouldn't become discouraged that every day we negotiate with competing identity structures. The struggle is part of the formation process, and growing patiently is the journey. Our soul struggles simply remind us that we are under reconstruction by a Savior who treasures us.

Don't be embarrassed by a collapsing weak identity. Simply repent, rejoice, and keep walking forward in grace.

The are many gospel-shaped people in the Bible whose stories we haven't explored—Tabitha, Silas, Aquila, Priscilla, Titus, Epaphras, Timothy, Luke, and others. Each of them was as common as you or me, and each of them was redefined by the gospel and providentially used by God. They struggled forward, growing slowly, and imperfectly living out the love they were given. Their journey required patient cultivation, just as ours.

THINK ON THESE THINGS

Daily identity formation has a nucleus—how we *think,* how we converse with ourselves. Purposefully feeding and directing our internal conversation is critical. Preach the gospel to yourself every day. Perpetually remind yourself who you are in Jesus. Paul challenged Corinthian believers, "For though we walk in the flesh, we are not waging war according to the flesh. For the weapons of our warfare are not of the flesh but have divine power to

destroy strongholds. We destroy arguments and every lofty opinion raised against the knowledge of God, and take every thought
captive to obey Christ" (2 Cor. 10:3–5).

He told Timothy to give his whole attention to these things
(1 Tim. 4:13–15).

Our inner narrative shapes the development of our hearts. A
gospel identity grows as we learn to captivate thoughts to God's
truth, continually reframing our hearts in gospel realities.

Paul learned and taught this:

> Do not be anxious about anything, but in everything
> by prayer and supplication with thanksgiving let your
> requests be made known to God. And the peace of
> God, which surpasses all understanding, will guard your
> hearts and your minds in Christ Jesus.
>
> Finally, brothers, whatever is true, whatever is honor-
> able, whatever is just, whatever is pure, whatever is love-
> ly, whatever is commendable, if there is any excellence,
> if there is anything worthy of praise, think about these
> things. What you have learned and received and heard
> and seen in me—practice these things, and the God of
> peace will be with you. (Phil. 4:6–9)

• • •

I walked into Old City Jerusalem again this morning. It was
chilly, so I looked for a place outside in the sun to sit and write. It
wasn't long before I was warm enough to remove my jacket and
roll up my sleeves. It reminded me of an Aesop's fable.

Sun and Wind engage in a contest to see who could cause a man
to remove his coat the fastest. Wind took his turn first, blustering

and blowing, but the harder Wind blew, the more tightly the man clung to his coat. Finally, Wind gave up, and it was Sun's turn.

Sun simply shined—brighter and warmer—gently and gradually warming the man until he voluntarily, willingly removed his coat. What the Wind could not do by force, the Sun accomplished easily by warmth.[4]

This is how God shapes our gospel identity. He doesn't coerce; He wins us. He never blusters us into a mold; He warms us gently into His image. Once you experience His love, you simply trust Him—you want to love Him and want to follow Him.

As a result of following Him, He leads you to places you never imagined. He leads you through valleys that you hope to never return to, through seasons that are complex, painful, and confusing. But in all of His leading, He's warming. He is ever loving you closer to Himself, never giving up, never casting you aside, never taking His undivided attention and tender compassion off of you.

Through it all, you would never undo it. The work He does makes even the hardest places of the journey worth it. He holds you together, which makes you love and trust Him all the more.

A gospel identity is that which has come to love and trust God so much it simply desires to discard whatever stands in His way. Religion characterizes God more like the wind—blustering and billowing into your life with effacing demands, threatening you to comply.

In my experience, He's more like the sun, gently warming us toward Himself. Your circumstances may billow in life, but Jesus quietly grounds you and sustains you. He describes Himself as Shepherd, Refuge, Father, Mediator, Provider, Protector, Deliverer —Savior. He won't oppress you into bondage. He loves you into safety.

As you turn the page to the conclusion, I want to share something God reminded me about on a street corner in New York one winter evening.

"Put on the new self, which is being renewed
in knowledge after the image of its creator."

COLOSSIANS 3:10

CONCLUSION

Live Your Story in His Story

"Like newborn infants, long for the
pure spiritual milk, that by it you may grow up."

1 PETER 2:2

THE WINTER AIR bit at our lungs as we walked at an energized pace through the city—New York in the winter. Steam rose from the manhole covers, horns honked, brake lights lined the streets like long strands of Christmas decor. Focused people briskly walked toward destinations unknown, in every direction. We were surrounded by skyscrapers as many cultures and ages meshed together in buildings and smells and people all around us. On one corner, a man cooked kabobs on a cart; on another, a lady sold beanies; and on another, a police officer directed traffic. Shops and restaurants were filled, and the vapor of our breaths could be seen as we walked. Our conversation ranged from writing to Broadway to the gospel.

There are few things I enjoy more than taking Haylee, my young adult daughter, to New York City. For us, it's an escape from normal into organized chaos. We love the culture-shift from our more suburban home in Connecticut. The city distracts our minds, engages our imaginations, and spurs on conversation. And we most love to walk it. Trains and cabs inhibit the experience. Walking the city lets you absorb it.

Not long ago, knowing she would be leaving for college soon, we went into the city with tickets to a show. Arriving just in time, I presented my ticket to the security guard, who told me that my backpack was not permitted. This was an immediate problem as there was no place to store my computer and no time to figure it out. Reluctantly, I looked at my daughter and the two others with us and said, "Go ahead without me. I'll hang out, do some work, and catch you guys afterwards." It pained them to go without me, but there was no time to deal with emotions or work it out. So they reluctantly went in, and I waited.

Minutes later, I was about to buy a cup of coffee and grab a seat when my phone rang. It was Haylee.

"Hey, where are you?"

"I'm in the lobby."

With that, she turned the corner, and her face lit up as my heart melted a little. I realized she had left the show to be with me.

"What are you doing?" I asked. "You came to see the show!"

"No, I came to spend time with you. I don't care about the show. Let's go."

With that, we ventured into the cold night air, ready for another walk in the city. Conversation meandered from school, to family, to boys, to college, to writing, to life in general. Though a college student, Haylee still hadn't outgrown hangin' with Dad, and holding especially tightly to his arm when walking the city on a cold night.

I'll never forget what she said that night as we paused, waiting for a crosswalk light to change. She shivered, let out a sigh, squeezed my arm, and delightedly said, "Oh, I just love New York City!"

My throat tightened. Tears warmed my eyes as God reminded me—*I knew she would.*

Instantly, my mind sort of time-warped back to 2012. I had just completed my one-year battle with cancer, and God was orchestrating that next huge transition for our family—West Coast to East Coast, large ministry to small ministry, warm weather to cold weather, assistant pastor to senior pastor. My fears were overwhelming in that season. My identity was uprooted, and no fear was more powerful than how the transition would impact my family.

Though clearly providential, the ordeal was extremely difficult for all of us, but none more than Haylee. Her life was upended, resulting in much emotional turmoil that year. Life was frazzled, frustrating, and often combustible. It was hard enough for her to become a teenager, but it became worse when an unexpected move was thrown in.

And yet, there was a core durability in our hearts, a truth underneath the surface chaos—*God brought us to this place.* Although well shaken, our family identity in Jesus was intact. Those first two years, we continually returned to Jesus as our ultimate reference point. All other anchor points had been sovereignly removed. Wonderfully, God never failed to prove Himself and His presence in it all.

I recalled a dark night and a long walk in the rain when I wept and told God, "I came here in obedience to You, but I don't want to lose or hurt my family in the process." He reminded me that He loves them far more than I could.

Then my mind replayed another hard conversation with Haylee. "Haylee, if you will surrender and trust God in this, two years from now you won't want your old life back. God has blessings in mind for you that you have yet to experience!" Neither of us could see it then.

Not long after that conversation, she surrendered her will to God's, and peace returned to her junior-high heart.

Standing on the street corner that night, six years later, I smiled at Haylee after she expressed how much she loved New York City. I patted her hand, and echoed that earlier reminder from God. "He knew you would!"

"Who?"

"Jesus. He knew your heart. He planned this. He brought you here, and you let Him. He took away your old life and gave you a new one, and now you love where He brought you. You wouldn't go back to your old self, would you?"

"Nope." She smiled with full satisfaction. "Not ever. I love what God did in our lives."

She couldn't see it, but the lump in my throat expanded, and I quietly said, "Thank You, Lord."

We continued walking, talking, celebrating, cherishing each other, and thanking God for His good plans. Sometimes they are painful—*losing* is painful. Sometimes they are disorienting—*finding* is confusing. But always, guaranteed, for sure, every time, His paths end in *celebrating* and *flourishing*. It's who He is. It's what He does. It's His A-game!

He creates flourishing hearts and eternal celebrations—not just someday in heaven, but right now in this messy here and now. He prepares a celebration feast in the middle of the war, not only after it's won (Ps. 23:5). He brings good cheer in the middle of the storm, not only when it's past (Matt. 14:27).

• • •

I chose to write this book using stories as much as possible because that's how God does His work. Knowledge informs us, but stories shape us—and stories are what we live. Each of us is not only writing or living a story, but because of the gospel, we have new stories that are written into a much larger, truer story.

Go into the story, and live it out. Frame your life in God's story, and make Him the center of yours. I heard Al Andrews recently say, "Know your story. If you don't, your story will live you."[1]

Chances are, when you picked up this book, your story was living you. Perhaps you felt powerless—swept up by whatever has happened to you, lost in the swirling torrents of uncontrollable circumstances, and maybe wondering if you have a story worth living. In a gospel identity, you can begin living *your* story. The story no longer has control, and you don't need control—because your Savior is in control.

Your story unfolds in His. You are His. He is yours. And the best chapters in your story are still ahead.

Over and over, **run home** rather than give up in failure; **face upward** rather than head down in hardship; **stand up** in confident faith rather than floundering in fear; **embrace smallness** rather than pursuing a large self; **bleed grace** in hurtful or sensitive relational situations; **fall down** before His presence in authentic worship rather than serving in your own strength; and **grow forward** through patient cultivation.

Every day, choose to stop trying to achieve your self. Believe and receive the self that only Jesus can provide. Watch God weave

His beautiful, eternal gospel story into the fibers of your smaller, fragile story. Immerse your heart into experiencing Jesus and His gospel. As you understand how loved you are, you will love in return. Love builds trust, and trust flows into obedient service and true success.

This is who you really are. Jesus says so! He knows what you love and how to make you full. Rest in His definitions, for only He knows how to take you all the way home.

Follow Jesus, my friend.

You're going to flourish, and I would love to hear about it. I wish you God's best as you grow into your gospel-shaped self.

"So we do not lose heart. Though our
outer self is wasting away, our inner self
is being renewed day by day."

2 CORINTHIANS 4:16

THE FOLLOWING CHART is identical to the one earlier in the book, except we've now added the third column of contrasting qualities of a gospel identity.

Traditional Identity	Modern Identity	Gospel Identity
Others define me	I define me	Jesus defines me
I am what I do	I am what I desire	I am who God created
Who I am supposed to be	Who I want to be	Who I am designed to be
Be who others say	Be who I say	Be who Jesus designed
Value community	Value individuality	Value both
Looks outward	Looks inward	Looks upward
Begins outside, works in	Begins inside, works out	Begins upward, works inward, then out
Live responsibly	Live adventurously	Live both
Pursue duty	Pursue dreams	Pursue both in one call
External validation	Internal validation	Eternal validation
Seek affirmation	Demand affirmation	Receive infinite affirmation
Performance-driven	Desire-driven	Love-driven
Substantive	Mystical	Truthful, spiritual
Hard work	Self-discovery	Restful discovery
Others focused	Self-focused	Jesus-focused
Sacrificial, honorable	Greedy, demanding	Generous from fullness
Lose myself to others	Lose myself to me	Lose myself to Jesus
Altruistic	Individualistic	Lovingly both
Fit in	Stand out	Perfectly placed
Be usual	Be exceptional	Be restfully real
Achieve your *self*	Discover your *self*	Receive your *self*

Traditional Identity	Modern Identity	Gospel Identity
Construct your *self*	Create your *self*	Grow into your *self*
Follow directions	Follow dreams	Follow Jesus
Keep the rules	Break the rules	Trust the love of the rule Giver
Reinforce the rules	Run from the rules	Enjoy the relationship
Comply to a system	Defy the system	Trade the system for a Person
Live up to standards	Live for personal passions	Live from abundant life
Do what is noble	Do what feels good	Do as gospel desires lead
Love to be affirmed	Love to gratify self	Love because you are loved
Give obligated love	Seek self-serving love	Give the infinite love you've received
Give to get	Give to feel good	Give from love for Jesus
Ought to serve	Feels good to serve	Love and want to serve

BELOW IS A SUMMARY of what we've studied about a gospel identity that may prove helpful as you consider the big-picture concepts of allowing Jesus to define you.

Flourishing in a Gospel Identity
"View every life circumstance through the lens of gospel reality."

How God Uses Life Experience to Shape Gospel Identity

- He calls us to repent in failure.

- He lifts our heads in hardship.

- He stabilizes our fears with solid ground.

- He shows us big value in small assignments.

- He enables us to bleed grace in difficult relationships.

How We Patiently Cultivate Gospel Identity

- We fall down in worship—practicing His presence every day.

- We serve in love—fulfilling His mission to bless others.

- We grow in grace—patiently maturing in the gospel for the rest of our lives.

It will take the rest of my life to become who I really am. It begins by believing, grows through experiencing, and matures with patient cultivating.

Acknowledgments

THE STORY OF THIS BOOK was a precise answer to prayer, and as a result, the thanks could be longer than the book! This project was very much a team effort, and I am grateful to every friend that encouraged it forward. My gratitude is overflowing toward those who most closely influenced the project:

My Family—First, thank you for patiently enduring the long process of my spiritual formation though all these years. Dana, thank you for encouraging me to "not give up" on writing and for celebrating this project with me. Lance (and Hillarie), thank you for making the first trip to Moody with me and for energetically believing that it would happen. Larry (and Mariah), thank you for letting me use your story to strengthen others and for encouraging me many times along the way. Haylee, thank you for loving books and for joyfully and creatively contributing throughout the whole process.

My Team and Church Family—Thank you to our Emmanuel staff and family for growing together, and for laboring in the harvest fields of New England with us. Thank you for loving our family and for encouraging me to embrace writing and to step through the open doors that God provides.

My Assistant—Thank you, Ashlee Dickerson, for your tireless and joyful reading and rereading of this manuscript over the course of a year. Your constructive input is woven into every page.

The Moody Publishers Team—Thank you to Paul Santhouse for extending an invitation into the Moody family. Thank you to Tim Sisk (Moody faculty) for your friendship and encouragement in writing. Thank you to Amy Simpson for your belief in this project, and for your amazing editing and coaching at every point of the journey. Thank you to Amanda Cleary Eastep for your awesome combination of ninja editing skills and timely humor. Thank you to each servant at Moody who labored to bring this book into the world. I am honored and grateful to serve Jesus with you all, and I am truly thankful for the friendships we have formed.

My Agent—Cynthia Ruchti, your godly and joyful spirit has impacted my life deeply. You have not only been a fantastic agent, but you have been a delightful friend and encourager. I thank God for bringing you into my life when He did. Thank you for welcoming me into the Books and Such Literary Agency. You were a direct answer to very specific prayer!

NOTES

Chapter 1—Trying Hard

1. This quote is from my gracious friend Thomas McMillan, who shared it with the Emmanuel Baptist Church family on Sunday morning, June 14, 2020, as we shared a conversation together about prejudice and secular identity narratives. Thomas McMillan, "Worldview Reset: Seeing Each Other through God's Lens," Conversation with Cary Schmidt, Part 3 of *Reset* sermon series, June 14, 2020, at Emmanuel Baptist Church in Newington, CT, https://ebcnewington.com/messages/reset/?sapurl=Lyt4NHJzL2xiL21pLyt6cTVxNDRnP2VtYmVkPXRydWU=.

2. The first person who ever addressed the "source of self" in my spiritual journey was author (and now my friend) David F. Wells in his books *The Courage to Be Protestant* and *God in the Whirlwind*. Dr. Wells's writings were wonderfully influential in my growing understanding of the things I wrote about in this book. David F. Wells, *God in the Whirlwind: How the Holy-love of God Reorients Our World* (Wheaton, IL: Crossway, 2014), and *The Courage to Be Protestant: Reformation Faith in Today's World* (Wheaton, IL: Crossway, 2014).

Chapter 2—Splinterville

1. C. S. Lewis, *The Four Loves* (San Francisco: HarperOne, 2017), loc. 1689 of 2066, Kindle.

2. Neil T. Anderson, *Who I Am in Christ* (Bloomington, MN: Bethany House, 2014), ch. 25, loc. 1989 of 3169, Kindle.

3. I developed this list beginning with a list of eleven identity markers outlined in Brian Rosner's book *Known by God: A Biblical Theology of Personal Identity, Biblical Theology for Life* (Grand Rapids: Zondervan, 2017), 41. I added my own commentary based upon my personal ministry experiences, as well as adding the following factors to the list: power/status, love/romance, past abuse/victimization, failures/regrets, social media/fake identity, function/abilities.

Chapter 3—Weak Identity

1. This farewell is offered to audience members at the end of the "Happily Ever After" fireworks show, Disney World's Magic Kingdom, Orlando, FL, debuted 2017. "Happily Ever After (Magic Kingdom)," Disney Parks Script Central, March 20, 2018, http://www.disneyparkscripts.com/happily-ever-after-magic-kingdom/.

2. David Shimer, "Yale's Most Popular Class Ever: Happiness," *New York Times*, January 26, 2018, https://www.nytimes.com/2018/01/26/nyregion/at-yale-class-on-happiness-draws-huge-crowd-laurie-santos.html.

3. James Baldwin, "An Interview with James Baldwin," interview by Studs Terkel (*Almanac*, WFMT, Chicago: December 29, 1961) in *James Baldwin: The Last Interview and Other Conversations* (New York: Melville House, 2014), loc. 95 of 1439, Kindle.

4. "A Million Dreams," *The Greatest Showman*, directed by Michael Gracey, music by Benj Pasek and Justin Paul (Los Angeles: 20th Century Fox, 2017).

5. David Wells, personal conversation, January 7, 2019.

6. "2018 Cigna U.S. Loneliness Index," Cigna, *Multivu*, May 2018, https://www.multivu.com/players/English/8294451-cigna-us-loneliness-survey/docs/IndexReport_1524069371598-173525450.pdf.

7. Jules Schroeder, "Millennials, This Is What Your Quarter-Life Crisis Is Telling You," *Forbes*, September 8, 2016, https://www.forbes.com/sites/julesschroeder/2016/09/08/millennials-this-is-what-your-quarter-life-crisis-is-telling-you/#360122f63262.

8. David G. Myers, *The American Paradox: Spiritual Hunger in an Age of Plenty* (New Haven, CT: Yale University Press, 2000), back cover.

9. Kirsten Weir, "Worrying Trends in U.S. Suicide Rates," *American Psychological Association* 50, no. 3 (2019): 24, https://www.apa.org/monitor/2019/03/trends-suicide.

10. Melissa Healy, "Suicide Rates for U.S. Teens and Young Adults Are the Highest on Record," *Los Angeles Times*, June 18, 2019, https://www.latimes.com/science/la-sci-suicide-rates-rising-teens-young-adults-20190618-story.html.

11. Allan Bloom, *The Closing of the American Mind: How Higher Education Has Failed Democracy and Impoverished the Souls of Today's Students* (New York: Simon & Schuster, 2008), 76 of 574, Scribd.

12. Leo Tolstoy, *A Confession*, translated by Aylmer Maude (Mineola, NY: Dover Publications, 2005), 27–32 of 111, Scribd.

13. David F. Wells, *The Courage to Be Protestant: Reformation Faith in Today's World*, 2nd ed. (Grand Rapids: Eerdmans, 2017), 135.

14. Charles Taylor, *Sources of the Self: The Making of the Modern Identity* (Cambridge, MA: Harvard University Press, 1989), 1–24.

15. The first person I heard teach on identity was Tim Keller. In this text, he is quoted directly several times, but it is appropriate to say his biblical insight (as well as the insights of others) through writing and teaching was influential in many of the concepts shared in this manuscript.

Chapter 4—Traditional Identity

1. *Frozen*, directed by Chris Buck and Jennifer Lee, music by Robert Lopez and Kristen Anderson-Lopez (Burbank, CA: Walt Disney Animation Studios, 2013).

2. *The Lion King*, directed by Roger Allers and Rob Minkoff, music by Elton John and Tim Rice (Burbank, CA: Walt Disney Animation Studios, 1994).

3. *Beauty and the Beast*, directed by Gary Trousdale and Kirk Wise, music by Howard Ashman and Alan Menken (Burbank, CA: Walt Disney Animation Studios, 1991). *Moana*, directed by Ron Clements and John Musker, music by Lin-Manuel Miranda, Opetaia Foa'i, and Mark Mancina (Burbank, CA: Walt Disney Animation Studios, 2016). *Aladdin*, directed by Ron Clements and John

Musker; music by Tim Rice, Alan Menken, and Howard Ashman (Burbank, CA: Walt Disney Animation Studios, 1992). *The Little Mermaid*, directed by Ron Clements and John Musker, music by Howard Ashman and Alan Menken (Burbank, CA: Walt Disney Animation Studios, 1989).

4. *Toy Story*, directed by John Lasseter, music by Randy Newman (Emeryville, CA: Pixar Animation Studios, 1995).

5. Derek Thompson, "Workism Is Making Americans Miserable," *Atlantic*, February 24, 2019, https://www.theatlantic.com/ideas/archive/2019/02/religion-workism-making-americans-miserable/583441/.

6. Jordan B. Peterson, *12 Rules for Life: An Antidote to Chaos* (Toronto: Penguin Random House Canada, 2018), Kindle.

7. Thompson, "Workism Is Making Americans Miserable."

8. Thomas McMillan, "Worldview Reset: Seeing Each Other through God's Lens," conversation with Cary Schmidt, Part 3 of *Reset* sermon series, June 14, 2020, at Emmanuel Baptist Church in Newington, CT, https://ebcnewington.com/messages/reset/?sapurl=Lyt4NHJzL2xiL21pLyt6cTVxNDRnP2VtYmVkPX RydWU=.

9. *Star Wars: Episode IV – A New Hope*, directed by George Lucas (San Francisco: Lucasfilm; distributed by 20th Century Fox, 1977).

10. *Toy Story*, directed by John Lasseter.

11. "I Will Go Sailing No More" by Randy Newman, track 3 on *Toy Story* (soundtrack), Walt Disney Records, 1995.

Chapter 5—Modern Identity

1. Paul Trachtman, "A Brief History of Dada," *Smithsonian*, May 2006, https://www.smithsonianmag.com/arts-culture/dada-115169154.

2. Joseph Loconte, *A Hobbit, A Wardrobe, and a Great War* (Nashville: Nelson Books, 2015), ix–26.

3. Trachtman, "A Brief History of Dada."

4. Charles Taylor, *Sources of the Self: The Making of the Modern Identity* (Cambridge, MA: Harvard University Press, 1989).

5. *Dear Evan Hansen,* music and lyrics by Benj Pasek and Justin Paul, Music Box Theatre, New York, December 2016.

6. "Let It Go" by Robert Lopez and Kristen Anderson-Lopez, track 5 on *Frozen* (Original Motion Picture Soundtrack), Walt Disney Records, 2013.

7. *For the First Time in Forever: A Frozen Sing-Along Celebration*, Disney's Hollywood Studios, Orlando, FL, debuted July 5, 2014.

8. Eugene Park, "Kanye West: From 'I Am a God' to 'Jesus Is King,'" The Gospel Coalition, October 28, 2019, https://www.thegospelcoalition.org/article/kanye-west-god-jesus-king.

9. Matt Smethurst, Timothy and Kathy Keller, "Tim and Kathy Keller on Dating, Marriage, Complementarianism, and Other Small Topics," The Gospel Coalition, October 24, 2019, https://www.thegospelcoalition.org/article/tim-kathy-keller-marriage.

10. Pam Grossman, "Yes, Witches Are Real. I Know Because I Am One," *Time*, May 30, 2019, https://time.com/5597693/real-women-witches.

11. Joshua Knobe, "In Search of the True Self," *New York Times*, June 5, 2011, https://opinionator.blogs.nytimes.com/2011/06/05/in-search-of-the-true-self/?searchResultPosition=9.

12. William Ernest Henley, "Invictus," Poetry Foundation, 1888, https://www.poetryfoundation.org/poems/51642/invictus.

PART TWO—FINDING

1. G. K. Chesterton, *Orthodoxy* (New York: John Lane Company, 1908), 35–36.

2. Oswald Chambers, "A Bond-Slave of Jesus," *My Utmost for His Highest*, November 3, 2019, https://utmost.org/classic/a-bond-slave-of-jesus-classic.

3. Ibid.

Chapter 6—Losing to Find

1. C. S. Lewis, *A Grief Observed* (originally published in 1961 under the pseudonym "N. W. Clerk") (New York: HarperCollins, 2009), loc. 569 of 860, Kindle.

2. *Strong's Concordance*, Bible Hub, s.v. "*bios*," #979, https://biblehub.com/str/greek/979.htm.

3. *Strong's Concordance*, Bible Hub, s.v. "*zoe*," #2222, https://biblehub.com/str/greek/2222.htm.

4. *Strong's Concordance*, Bible Hub, s.v. "*psuche*," #5590, https://biblehub.com/greek/5590.htm.

5. The story of the woman at the well is found in John 4.

6. Oswald Chambers, "The Commission of the Call," *My Utmost for His Highest*, September 30, 2019, https://utmost.org/classic/the-commission-of-the-call-classic.

Chapter 7—Jesus' Loss

1. *The Lord of the Rings* (film series), directed by Peter Jackson, based on the trilogy written by J. R. R. Tolkien (Burbank, CA: New Line Cinema, 2001–2003).

2. *Star Wars: Episode IV – A New Hope*, directed by George Lucas (San Francisco: Lucasfilm; distributed by 20th Century Fox, 1977).

3. I'm grateful for the writings and teachings of both Tim Keller and David F. Wells in introducing clarity to my theological understanding of God's holiness and

love, and how the narrative of Scripture brings them together in Jesus on the cross.

4. Timothy and Kathy Keller, *The Meaning of Marriage: Facing the Complexities of Commitment with the Wisdom of God* (New York: Penguin Books, 2011), 48.

5. Timothy Keller (@timkellernyc), ". . . Whatever it will cost you to be with God is nothing compared to what it cost Him to be with you," Twitter, November 26, 2016, 2:30 p.m, https://twitter.com/timkellernyc/status/802595318550429696.

Chapter 8—Gospel Identity

1. "Sep 12, 490 BCE: Battle of Marathon," *National Geographic*, July 28, 2014, http://ipod-ngsta.test.nationalgeographic.org/thisday/sep12/battle-marathon/.

2. *Strong's Exhaustive*, Bible Hub, s.v. "*euaggelion*," #2098, https://biblehub.com/str/greek/2098.htm.

Chapter 9—Run Home

1. Robert H. Thune and Will Walker, *The Gospel-Centered Life: Study Guide with Leader's Notes* (Greensboro, NC: New Growth Press, 2011), 20–26.

Chapter 10—Face Upward

1. Annie Dillard, *Pilgrim at Tinker Creek* (New York: HarperCollins Publishers, 2009), 41 of 315, Scribd.

Chapter 12—Embrace Smallness

1. *The Lord of the Rings* (film series), directed by Peter Jackson, based on the trilogy written by J.R.R. Tolkien (Burbank, CA: New Line Cinema, 2001–2003).

2. Irenaeus, *Five Books of St. Irenaeus Bishop of Lyons: Against Heresies with the Fragments That Remain of His Other Works*, translated by John Keble (Edinburgh, Scotland: CrossReach Publications, 2018), 301 of 3387, Scribd.

Chapter 13—Bleed Grace

1. Jennifer Emily, "Two Stunning Hugs End Amber Guyger's Murder Trial on a Merciful Note," *Dallas Morning News*, October 2, 2019, https://www.dallasnews.com/news/2019/10/02/two-stunning-hugs-end-amber-guygers-trial-merciful-note.

2. Ibid.

3. Brandt Jean, "'I Forgive You': Botham Jean's Brother Hugs Amber Guyger after She Gets 10 years in Prison," 204th District Court, Dallas, TX. Uploaded

to YouTube by *Dallas Morning News* on October 2, 2019, 0:4:12, https://www.youtube.com/watch?v=qeESVLQK4hw.

4. Ibid.

5. Tammy Kemp, "Judge Hugs Jean's Family, Guyger after Sentencing," 204th District Court, Dallas, TX. Uploaded to YouTube by AP Archive on October 7, 2019, 0:1:34, https://www.youtube.com/watch?v=kyKDSnKKl7M&t=22s.

6. Emily, "Two Stunning Hugs," October 2, 2019.

7. Ibid.

Chapter 15—Grow Forward

1. Oswald Chambers, "Diffusiveness of Life," *My Utmost for His Highest*, September 6, 2019, https://utmost.org/classic/diffusiveness-of-life-classic.

2. Oswald Chambers, "Springs of Benignity," *My Utmost for His Highest*, September 7, 2019, https://utmost.org/classic/diffusiveness-of-life-classic.

3. J. I. Packer, *Rediscovering Holiness: Know the Fullness of Life with God* (Grand Rapids: BakerBooks, 2009), loc. 498 of 4575, Kindle.

4. Attributed to Aesop, "The North Wind and the Sun," *Aesop's Fables*, translated by George Fyler Townsend (New York: HarperCollins, 2012), 260 of 410, Scribd.

Conclusion

1. Al Andrews, interview by Donald Miller, "10 Things Powerful People Can Do to Not Screw Up Their Lives," *Building a StoryBrand* (podcast), http://buildingastorybrand.com/episode-64.